Praise for

Longing to Belong

"As one who has longed to belong, I have looked for books that address the ever-present neediness in my heart. Thankfully, Shawna Marie Bryant's biblical scholarship, encouragement, and empathy offers a Jesus-honoring path toward wholeness. Bryant has taken the journey before us. She loves Jesus. And she loves you, her reader. Whether you study this alone or with a group of friends, I'm convinced you'll close the book loved, changed, and inspired."

—**Mary DeMuth,** author of *Healing Every Day*

"*Longing to Belong* comes from such a personal place in Shawna. She is a shining example of someone who decided the pain of rejection was not going to keep her down and defeated. By embracing the truths found in Psalm 139, Shawna gives the reader a transformational guide to freedom."

—**Joni Oquist,** Women's Pastor at Peoples Church, Fresno, California

"Shawna is someone I have come to know as both a gifted communicator and a person who strives to hear and be led by the Holy Spirit. I think highly not only of her talents and gifts but also of her and her family."

—**Dale Oquist,** Lead Pastor at Peoples Church, Fresno, California

"*Longing to Belong* is a beautiful, life-giving stroll through the powerful, nurturing, and life-transforming words of Psalm 139."

—**Pam Farrel,** Codirector of love-wise.com and author of the bestseller *Men Are Like Waffles, Women Are Like Spaghetti*

"God has given Shawna Marie Bryant a wonderful gift in teaching, and has called her to the ministry of teaching the Word of God to women. Shawna needs to be doing this. This is what she was created to do!"

—**David Jeremiah,** Founder and President of Turning Point Ministries, and Senior Pastor of Shadow Mountain Community Church

"In *Longing to Belong,* Shawna Marie Bryant embraces readers as good friends. She captures the pain of rejection and the certainty of hope. Through relatable, personal experiences and biblical stories, Shawna takes you step-by-step to the truth of acceptance. This is a resource you will refer to time and again."

—**Penelope Childers,** coauthor of *A Cry of the Heart*

"As pastor to a United States president, my dad, Rev. Michael Wenning, was considered a somebody. Somebodies get to endorse powerful books like this, filled with wisdom for broken hearts. As a nobody-knows-who, my opinion (and a few bucks) can buy you coffee! But maybe you need to hear from ordinary me, because after reading this book you will know beyond a shadow of a doubt how deeply, how widely, God adores you. And the best part? That makes you a pretty big somebody too!"

—**Andi Wenning Bull,** pastor, Bible teacher, and women's mentor

"Shawna Marie Bryant guides with grace and fresh insight. Her wisdoms are breaths of fresh air. Her continual direction back to the one who sets us apart and keeps us in his belonging points readers to the source of everything they need. Shawna's book is a timely and important work. I highly recommend *Longing to Belong.*"

—**Jami Amerine,** author of *Sacred Ground, Sticky Floors*

"With honesty and vulnerability, Shawna Marie Bryant shares her journey of discovery. You'll join the 'I'm Special Sisterhood' and walk the path of acceptance, unlocking life-changing doors. A must-read, especially if you are feeling 'less than,' because God considers you his masterpiece."

—**Barb Boswell,** author of *Every Time I Turn Around,*
God Whispers in My Ear!

"*Longing to Belong* is a fascinating account of how deeply God loves and cares for us. As you read this book, you will see yourself the way God sees you. Shawna Marie Bryant masterfully conveys the heart of our heavenly father while walking you through one of the most powerful Psalms ever written. I personally realized that when I embrace God's acceptance of me, self-acceptance becomes easier."

—**Ercell B. Charles,** President of Mentor Performance Systems, and Vice President of Customer Transformation at Dale Carnegie & Associates

"Life is difficult and sometimes overwhelming, but a practical, sincere, powerful book like this one by Shawna Marie Bryant brings hope. Shawna invites you to join her in a sisterhood of learning and leaning into the Word of God together, using one of my favorite Psalms. Her guide to journaling through life's ups and downs is something I will treasure, use in my own life, and share with others."

—**Penny Murray,** Director of Women's Ministry at NorthPark Community Church, Fresno, California

LONGING TO
BELONG

LONGING TO
BELONG

Discovering the Joy of Acceptance

SHAWNA MARIE BRYANT

LEAFWOOD
PUBLISHERS

an imprint of Abilene Christian University Press

LONGING TO BELONG
Discovering the Joy of Acceptance

LEAFWOOD
P U B L I S H E R S
an imprint of Abilene Christian University Press

Copyright © 2020 by Shawna Marie Bryant

ISBN 978-1-68426-480-3 | LCCN 2019057818

Printed in the United States of America

LIBRARY OF CONGRESS CATALOGING-IN-PUBLICATION DATA
Names: Bryant, Shawna Marie, 1962- author.
Title: Longing to belong : discovering the joy of acceptance / Shawna Marie Bryant.
Description: Abilene, Texas : Leafwood Publishers, [2020] | Includes
    bibliographical references.
Identifiers: LCCN 2019057818 | ISBN 9781684264803 (paperback)
Subjects: LCSH: Self-esteem—Religious aspects—Christianity. |
    Self-acceptance—Religious aspects—Christianity. | Bible. Psalms,
    CXXXIX—Commentaries.
Classification: LCC BV4598.24 .B78 2020 | DDC 248.4—dc23
LC record available at https://lccn.loc.gov/2019057818

Cover design by Thinkpen Design | Interior text design by Sandy Armstrong, Strong Design

Leafwood Publishers is an imprint of Abilene Christian University Press
ACU Box 29138, Abilene, Texas 79699

1-877-816-4455 | www.leafwoodpublishers.com

20 21 22 23 24 25 / 7 6 5 4 3 2 1

To the brave women who traveled this journey of discovery with me at Peoples Church Fresno, eager to walk in victory, and to my faithful prayer team who prayed for each of these women by name for weeks on end and prayed this book into your hands.

Contents

Chapter One

THE MANIFESTO

Sticks and stones may break my bones, but I don't believe the rest of that singsong. I wouldn't have written this book if words never hurt me. The Instagram caption says, "All of us having a blast!" My stomach churns because I wasn't invited. The Facebook post links a photo album labeled, "Backyard get together with family and close friends." My throat knots with the realization that I'm not considered close. My daughter screams, "I hate you! I don't want to live with you anymore!" My heart breaks as her criticism amplifies my fear of failure.

Contrary to this misguided singsong, words do have power. I believe the words we form with our tongues have so much power, they can give life or bring about death. Emotional stabs may not break bones, but they kill hopes and happiness. Words can also revive us after we have tasted the poison of despair. Are you ready to conquer joy-robbing jabs with a small but mighty weapon?

God has given you a one-of-a-kind sword with divine power. Nothing like the weapons of this world, your heaven-sent weapon was crafted to cut through lies and take thoughts captive. You can demolish the deathly effects of every debasing thought, word, or deed leveled against you by wielding your truth-infused tongue.

The book you are holding contains a Scripture-based Manifesto—a public declaration of intentions—that empowers you to speak life-giving affirmations. The Manifesto will be your weapon against every lie that schemes to devalue you. It will tickle your tongue with the tasty truth of how special you are. Let's call it the "Manifesto of Acceptance"; and make no mistake—it has divine power to demolish strongholds.

Declaring God's Word arms you with the sword of the Spirit. Forged from Psalm 139, the Manifesto of Acceptance turns your tongue into a sword. The seven simple sayings in the Manifesto pack a wallop. In your hands—or rather, from your mouth—these declarations become a mighty weapon. Between here and the last page of this book, you will soak in Psalm 139, grouped into sections that support a line from the Manifesto as follows:

Verses from Psalm 139	Manifesto of Acceptance
1–4	God knows me.
5–8	He is always with me.
9–12	I am not invisible.
13–16	I am wonderfully made.
17–18	God's countless thoughts are for me.
19–22	I have enemies, but . . .
23–24	I can walk in victory!

Declaring these seven lines will help silence the lies you've believed about your identity. These declarations will also help you focus on truth. Are you ready to take your thoughts captive? Captivity is a good thing when it comes to destructive thought patterns. You don't want them roaming freely through your mind, wreaking havoc on your sense of worth.

It's time to identify and renounce false beliefs. It's time to acknowledge and declare truth. It's time to claim your place of belonging. God's Word empowers your tongue to resuscitate hope and snuff out despair. Sticks and stones and emotional stabs all cause injury. But no foe can match the mighty sword of the Spirit— even if it's as tiny as your tongue.

I used to battle rejection, but now I believe what my Creator says about how valuable I am. Rejection may have trapped me behind enemy lines in the past, but it will never defeat me again. Not ever. Just saying it makes it so. I owe that win in a big way to Psalm 139, and I'm cheering you on to a similar victory. I believe you can rout rejection or any other enemy of your true identity. I believe you can discover the joy of acceptance. I sincerely do. With everything in me, I want you to believe it too. Believing is key. So is speaking. If you've got a tongue in your mouth, you already have what it takes to win this thing. And if you can't speak, I'm confident you can think. So we will start there.

Welcome to the *I'm Special Sisterhood*

When I taught this material at my home church, I began by greeting each brave woman who walked through the door of that Bible study classroom with a flower. I wish I could do the same for you. Will you play along with me? Reach out your hand, and receive a single, beautiful bloom. It's your favorite, so go ahead and take it. As you hold it and breathe in its fragrance, receive this as well: Welcome to the *I'm Special Sisterhood*.[1] You are beautiful. You belong. You are loved.

I realize that some of us have a hard time pondering the phrase "I'm special," let alone saying it out loud. Fortunately, my daughter Sarah has no trouble with the concept. When she was a little girl and I tucked her in at night, she always wanted me to scratch her back gently. I'm not sure how the ritual evolved from affectionate scratching to communicating, but I remember drawing letters on her back and pausing between words until she guessed what

I had spelled. I began with I. L-O-V-E. Y-O-U. Soon, when I'd scratch the letter I, Sarah would blurt out, "I know, Momma. I love you." One night, I decided to trick her and scratched A-M. S-P-E-C-I-A-L. I'll never forget the night she caught on to that phrase. As I started drawing the letter S, she declared, "I know. I know. I'm special." After that, I always found time to include that "mystery phrase," no matter how much she rolled her eyes. I wish I could say I strategized that scenario from the outset so my daughter would grow up believing and speaking the truth about how special she is. But to be honest, I was astonished the first time I heard her blurt out that declaration.

In the moments that followed, as I continued lightly scratching my daughter's back, I remembered a breakthrough scene I had witnessed as a recent college graduate serving as a high school camp counselor.

The door to my cabin of girls was ajar. I reached to push it open just as my best friend, Sharon, sternly exclaimed, "Say it! I want to hear you say it!"

Why was she in my cabin? Hers was next door. "I can't," came the weak reply. I recognized the voice of a darling girl in my cabin who rarely spoke. She was taller than me and gorgeous, with wavy brown hair and sad blue eyes. I had prayed to get through to her somehow.

"I can say it," Sharon said, a little softer this time. "I'm special. See? Now it's your turn."

I suddenly felt like I was eavesdropping on a significant encounter, but I couldn't help myself. I pressed gently on the door and peeked in. Sharon stood behind the teen with her hands firmly on the girl's shoulders. They were looking into the scratched and dingy mirror hanging above the chipped sink in the back corner of the cabin.

The girl shook her head. "I really can't."

Sharon would not have it. "You are special," she said. "It's true, and you need to believe it. I want to hear you say it."

I saw the teenager's shoulders rise and fall in a long, heavy sigh under the weight of her doubt and Sharon's hands. "You really think so?"

"I know so." Was the counselor from next door pretending to be stern? If so, she fooled me. I could never get away with that attitude. But it was working with this girl. "You are special, and I will hear you say it if it takes all day."

The girl giggled, and said, "I'm special."

"Say it again."

"I'm special."

"Say it louder!" Sharon nearly shouted.

"I'm special!" They laughed, and the joy was palpable.

"Now get back out there, and don't you forget it!"

I saw them turn toward me, and I dashed into Sharon's cabin. My wise and determined friend found me there, wiping my eyes. "You got through to her," I said. "I couldn't, but you did."

Sharon knew when to push and how. I wonder if I need to verbally march you over to your mirror. Can you say the words "I'm special"?

Please put your flower down for a minute so I can teach you the secret signal for the *I'm Special Sisterhood*. No, I haven't forgotten about the flower, and yes, I'm serious. I crafted this book to help you climb out of the pit of an unmet longing, and you can't do that by just quietly sitting there and reading. In fact, as you turn the pages you hold in your hands, you will continually collide with a call to action: believe and speak. My insistence on believing and speaking is firmly established in both the Old and New Testaments. According to 2 Corinthians 4:13, "It is written [in Psalm 116:10]: 'I believed; therefore I have spoken.' Since we have that same spirit of faith, we also believe and therefore speak" (NIV).

Some people speak with their hands—literally. I was astounded when I learned how to say "I'm special" in American Sign Language. The first time I saw it, goosebumps coursed from the back of my neck down my arms and back up again. I adopted it as our sign for the *I'm Special Sisterhood*. Before your precious head hits your pillow tonight, would you stand in front of the mirror and tell yourself how special you are? I'd love for you to practice the secret signal while saying "I'm special" out loud. If anybody sees you, you can honestly say you're learning a phrase in sign language.

To say "I'm" in sign language, you simply point to yourself midchest with the index finger of your right hand.

To sign "special," you first hold your right hand in front of you, pointing up with the same finger you just used to point to yourself. You should see your other fingers tucked under your thumb. Got it? Now, grab the tip of that index finger with the fingertips of your left hand, and pull it straight up a couple inches.[2] It's as if you're humbly holding out a little stick figure of yourself, and an outside force swoops in and lifts you up. I picture the hand of God reaching down from heaven to pull us out of the miry clay of insignificance.

When you slip on slimy lies, you can rise up and dust off by declaring truth—even if your declaration starts with silently signing "I'm special." Like the Manifesto of Acceptance, the secret signal will help you refocus on truth when feelings of insignificance highjack your thoughts and send your self-image into a death spiral. Speaking of the Manifesto, I look forward to guiding you through it line by line in the pages to come. I believe the Manifesto's seven simple declarations hold supernatural keys to freedom that will help you claim your place of belonging— your *rightful* place of belonging. I know these keys work because they opened my eyes to see myself as loved and accepted. They unlocked the truth of my extreme value and esteemed identity.

They exposed lies about my worth as empty words that wilt under the weight of God's promises. Finding and using these supernatural keys will do the same for you, sister. I hope you're OK with me calling you my sister. I meant what I said when I welcomed you to the *I'm Special Sisterhood* and gave you a virtual flower.

Merriam-Webster gives a three-part definition of "sisterhood." It first mentions the relationship of female siblings. Next, it references a religious community of sisters, especially a society of women in a religious order (like nuns). However, the final definition is what inspired the name for our community. Sisterhood also refers to the solidarity of women based on shared conditions, experiences, or concerns. Sisterhood speaks of the empathy women feel for other women.

I feel the pain of any woman wounded by words that belittle or demean. I want my sisters to bask in the joy of acceptance, which drives my motivation to write this book. Based on the fact that you picked it up and read this far, I'm confident that like me, you've tasted the conditions, experiences, and concerns of not being accepted. Can anyone honestly say they've never known rejection? We are in this together, sister. I'm not suggesting we form a misery-loves-company community. Rather, we belong to a fellowship of believers united in purpose to heal from emotional injuries and move forward.

Our solidarity goes beyond our shared longing to belong. Based on growing up with a sister who is practically a twin, raising a daughter into adulthood, working with women's ministry groups across the country, and being female, I'm convinced women share three deeply felt needs that leave an empty ache when we're not accepted: We want to be beautiful. We want to belong. And we want to be loved. I believe rejection strategically targets these vital needs to rob us of the assurance that Jesus already met them for us.

We Want to Be Beautiful

A television commercial came out several years ago that I spent way too much time thinking about. It bothered me so much that I finally had to ask myself why. The exotic model promoting the product (I think it was shampoo) opened the thirty-second advertisement saying, "Don't hate me because I'm beautiful." The obvious message of the commercial was if we bought whatever she was selling, we would be beautiful too. While I was annoyed that the advertiser defined beauty in such superficial terms, that lie was not what intensely bothered me. I hated the idea that a beautiful woman would assume other women would hate her just for being beautiful, and I hated that she could stare into the camera with such confidence while saying, "I'm beautiful" when I struggled to believe the same about myself. That stupid TV commercial got under my skin because it exposed a deep need and failed miserably at its promise to satisfy it.

We want to be beautiful, but rejection tells us our lips are too small or our nose is too big; our thighs are too round or our chest is too flat; our legs are too short or our feet are too long. God doesn't agree with these shallow, critical opinions, and neither should we. He created you and is well pleased with his handiwork. He told me so one day when I was thanking him for the beauty of Yosemite. I live nearby and make every effort to visit once a year. No matter how many times I see it, I will never grow tired of the glorious Tunnel View. I routinely applaud God and sing praises from my perch on the viewing wall, with El Capitan on the left, Bridal Veil Falls framed by The Three Sisters (Cathedral Rocks) on the right, and the magnificent Half Dome center stage. The day I heard from God on this matter, I happened to be singing a popular praise song about how he makes everything glorious. (I try to keep my voice down so I don't embarrass my family, or I wait until they are well out of earshot.) The chorus repeats a line three times. I sang and pointed to tall and proud El Capitan. "You made that glorious. Yep!" I sang and pointed to where the falls sent sparkly mist into the air. "Amen! That's glorious too." I pointed straight at Half Dome when I sang the line a third time about how he makes everything glorious. Then I felt in my spirit that I was supposed to point to myself and all the people taking in the same view (who may have heard my voice suddenly catch in my throat at the thought). Me? Glorious?

In that moment, God reminded me of the story of creation. In the beginning, God said, "Let there be light" and saw that the light was good. God created the land and the seas, and saw that it was good. God created the plants and the trees, and saw that it was good. God created the sun, moon, and stars, and saw that it was good. God created the creatures of the sea and the birds of the air, and saw that it was good. God created all the animals that move along the ground, and saw that it was good. Finally, God created mankind in his image. He created us—male and female—in his very own image. When he saw all he had made, did he see that it was good? After all, that's what he saw the first five days of creation. No, it wasn't good . . . not exactly. Not the day people first populated our planet.

God created male and female, looked around, and saw that it was *very* good. In other words, you are more glorious than all of Yosemite Valley!

Luke 4:16–17 tells us that one Sabbath day early in Jesus's ministry, he went to the synagogue in Nazareth and read from a scroll of the prophet Isaiah. After reciting a certain passage, "he rolled up the scroll, gave it back to the attendant and sat down." With all eyes locked on him, he said, "Today this scripture is fulfilled in your hearing" (Luke 4:20–21 NIV). Considering Jesus had just announced that the Spirit of the Lord was upon him and had anointed him to proclaim good news, recover sight for the blind, and set the oppressed free, you would think the people would've danced for joy. They actually did speak well of him at first, but only because he was their hometown hero. Jesus could see into their hearts and told them what was hidden there. They didn't like that one bit and drove him right out of town, intending to throw him off a cliff.

Rejected by those who knew him best, Jesus didn't let their treatment of him define him. The following Sabbath, he went to a synagogue in Capernaum, where he continued proclaiming, healing, and freeing. Jesus felt pain, and I'm convinced rejection from his family, friends, and neighbors that day in Nazareth hurt. But it didn't change the way he saw himself. Jesus knew what was written in Isaiah's scroll. If he hadn't stopped and rolled up the scroll when he did, but instead read the entirety of what we today call Isaiah 61, Jesus would've gotten to the part describing each of God's sons and daughters as "a planting of the LORD for the display of his splendor" (Isa. 61:3 NIV).

You are a display of God's splendor.

You might have an easier time planting yourself in the scene if you try picturing pure splendor first. Think of the distinction and magnificence of a king. The pomp and grandeur of a palace. The gorgeous appearance of a princess bride. Now imagine all that glorious brilliance shining on you—or even *from* you! Soak in the splendor, sister. Absorb it completely. You don't dimly flicker against the brilliance of prisms glittering off of Bridal Veil Falls. You don't pale in comparison to the majesty of God's creation. You don't fade away in the wash of light streaming from God's radiance. You, my friend, are a magnificent display of pure splendor.

Now, plant yourself in the splendor. Picture yourself reflecting the imposing pomp, brilliant distinction, and great brightness of God. You are beautiful. Don't just take my word for it. Your Creator says so. No matter what brand of shampoo you use, when God looks at you, what he sees is *very* good.

We Want to Belong

For too long, I thought I had to fit in to belong; but belonging isn't the same as fitting in. Trying to fit in where we don't belong inevitably magnifies our longing. When the world shuts me out, I find comfort knowing I don't belong to the world. Instead, I belong to the one who created it.

Jesus said, "If the world hates you, remember that it hated me first. The world would love you as one of its own if you belonged to it, but you are no longer part of the world. I chose you to come out of the world, so it hates you" (John 15:18–19).

Why do we try to fit in to a place Jesus chose us to come out of? My son Scott faced that dilemma soon after graduating high school. He moved away from the safety net of home and his circle of friends at a time when expressing differing views was considered hate speech. He attended classes near Berkeley while working part time as a barista for an extremely popular coffeehouse in the heart of San Francisco, where he encountered a wide array of people from a variety of backgrounds. Scott knew he didn't fit in, and he didn't try. He simply attended classes and served coffee with a smile—living in the world but not trying to fit in with the world. The Saturday before Scott's final exam, on one of his last days at work, my husband and I drove nearly four hours to San Francisco for a cup of coffee. Scott's manager and coworkers told us again and again what a great son we had, what a wonderful worker he was, and how much they were going to miss him. The week he arrived home, Scott was snatched up by a local coffeehouse owned by a Christian man who had established an environment that would invite God's manifest presence. When I asked my son if he enjoyed his new job, he said, "Yes. I *get* to talk about Jesus."

My son knew he belonged to something (and someone) greater than this world. That assurance helped him thrive even in places where he didn't fit in. I'm convinced his need to belong was met because Jesus prayed for him two thousand years before he was born. If you are a believer, Jesus prayed the same prayer over you. Yes, you! You'll find this prayer in John 17:9–20, which concludes with this: "I am praying not only for these disciples but also for all who will ever believe in me through their message."

Jesus knows the world hates believers because he chose us to come out of the world. That's why he prayed way back then for our protection today. He told the Father in heaven, "I'm not asking you to take them out of the world, but to keep them safe from the evil one. They do not belong to this world any more than I do."

Experiencing the lasting joy of acceptance in spite of shifting opinions about your worth depends on knowing your life is secure in Christ. Start by believing you belong to the one who loves you enough to lay down his life for you, and then ask the Father to lead you to a place where you fit in. After all, 1 John 5:14-15 says, "We are confident that he hears us whenever we ask for anything that pleases him. And since we know he hears us when we make our requests, we also know that he will give us what we ask for." So ask! Ask God to show you where you belong.

We Want to Be Loved

My husband, Steve, and I got married more than thirty years ago. Early on, during the honeymoon phase, he said something I knew wasn't true, and I called him on it. I had just told him I loved him, and he responded with, "I love you more." From where I stood, that wasn't possible. I grew up in a warm family of huggers and kissers. We expressed our love frequently and loudly. His family was far more reserved. They didn't holler "I lahhhhve youuuu" like mine did when a family member exited the building.

"No, I'm pretty sure I love you more," I said, thinking that would settle it, but he shook his head.

"I love you more."

That's when I got all philosophical on him. "You can't possibly love me more because I have a greater capacity to love."

He lifted his eyebrows. "Greater capacity?"

"Yes," I said, confident that would end it.

He laughed out loud, pointed to his heart, and said, "Greater capacity. Me more you." After that, he began to sign my birthday cards, Christmas cards, and anniversary cards with "Me more you," instead of "Love," before his name. That silly exchange carried us through an abundance of hard times when neither one of us had the capacity to love like God loves.

God's capacity to love is wide, long, high, and deep enough to embrace you, even in the deepest pit of your unmet longing. What greater longing does anyone have than to be loved? Here's the good news: God thinks you are so worthy of love that he willingly gave his only Son to prove it. Nothing you could ever do can make you unworthy of God's love. There's no better example than the author of Psalm 139. God's capacity to love is so great that he loved David—a man who took a married woman to bed, and when he learned she had conceived, schemed to cause her husband's death on the battlefield. David was an adulterous murderer, and yet he went down in history as a man after God's own heart.

If we believe we are unlovable, we will never know the truth about how powerful God's love is or grasp what it does for us. But when we understand how incredibly lovable we are to our Creator, rejection loses its sway over us. Do you know the children's song "Jesus Loves Me"? The lyrics call to mind a number of places where the Bible tells us that we are loved and that we belong. One of my favorites is 1 John 3:1 (NIV): "See what great love the Father has lavished on us, that we should be called children of God! And that is what we are! The reason the world does not know us is that it did not know him."

Jesus came down from heaven and fulfilled every prophecy spoken about him, from his birth in Bethlehem to his burial as a criminal. But the world didn't recognize him. The world still doesn't. And it doesn't always recognize how special you and I are either—probably because we don't belong here. Why chase after the love of the world when we are children of the Most High God? His love is high enough to fill us completely. His love is wide enough to keep us strong. His love satisfies our deepest longing. Not the love of another person, no matter how great their capacity may be.

There is no greater love than the love God has for you. I can almost hear him say, "Me more you."

Finding Your Key

I already told you that climbing out of the pit of an unmet longing requires more than quietly reading. Are you ready to move? Are you ready to search for your key to unlock the chains that bind you from belonging? I hope to challenge you along the way through this book and spur you on to victory. At times, I will ask you to silence lies by declaring truth. At times, I will invite you to study selected verses from Psalm 139 and write down what you learn. At times, I will appeal to your heart and mind with sketches about Bible characters who struggled with real issues.

I love the power of story. Storytelling captivates our thoughts and beckons us to a magical place of understanding. When we curl up with a good book, we can lose ourselves in someone else's circumstances, perhaps to take a break from our own. Good storytelling can help us return to reality with a fresh perspective. The Bible chronicles accounts of vulnerable people who were overlooked and underrated, and yet somehow discovered the joy of acceptance. You will meet characters as diverse as Joseph, who was born into privilege and sold into slavery, and Rahab, who survived the streets of a pagan culture to establish her name in the lineage of Israel's kings—from King David to King Jesus. My sketches of these and other Bible characters will help you identify with the honest struggles they faced and the hard lessons they learned.

A journal prompt follows each story, with a call to read and reflect on no more than four verses from Psalm 139 at a time. I implore you to climb out of that pit of unmet longing with a pen and some pages as your ladder. Journaling while meditating on short passages of the Bible helps me with right thinking (believing the truth) and right standing (speaking it out loud). After decades of filling journals during my private time of Bible study, I can testify to the substantial role this activity continues to play in transforming my mind and renewing my heart. Prayerfully working your way through the verses of David's beloved Psalm will fill your mind with truth.

The appendix contains instructions for a journaling method with five distinct steps:

1. Look
2. List
3. Learn
4. Listen
5. Live[3]

As you engage in each journaling activity, I pray you not only sense God's presence but also hear his still, small voice. I believe he has something to say to you.

I will guide your journaling and portion the Manifesto of Acceptance so it won't be a mouthful to memorize. You've already got a sword in your mouth and that's enough. Remember? The sword of the Spirit is the Word of God. I encourage you to take it out of its sheath by exercising your tongue. You'll learn—and declare—one short line of the Manifesto chapter by chapter to help reverse the destructive cycle of wrong thinking and wrong standing.

Would you take a moment right now to read all twenty-four verses of Psalm 139? Its message inspired the Manifesto, and I believe it holds supernatural keys to freedom. You will find the book of Psalms near the center of your Bible. As you read and reflect, God will reveal his love and care for you. He is eager to meet with you and tell you deep and mysterious things. Gaining greater understanding of his intimate knowledge of you, and opening up to receive his unconditional love for you, will satisfy your thirst for acceptance. So tuck a bookmark into this page and turn to your Bible—Psalm 139 to be exact.

While you're welcome to devour this book from cover to cover, I hope you'll take time to savor each chapter. As you absorb the stories, meditate on the scriptures, and apply the lessons, I believe God will reveal your key to freedom and equip you to walk in victory. No longer will disapproving opinions cast doubt on your inherent value. No longer will another's cold shoulder make you feel invisible. I believe this is your time to step up and reach for the key that will set you free. I suggest you start by marching over to a well-lit mirror, practicing our secret signal, and telling yourself how special you are. You are part of the *I'm Special Sisterhood*, and you've got what it takes to win. I believe in you, sister. Let's do this!

Chapter Two

GOD KNOWS ME

Psalm 139:1–4

¹ O Lord, you have examined my heart
and know everything about me.
² You know when I sit down or stand up.
You know my thoughts even when I'm far away.
³ You see me when I travel
and when I rest at home.
You know everything I do.
⁴ You know what I am going to say
even before I say it, Lord.

Counting the time I sent you to the mirror to practice our secret signal, the request I'm about to make amounts to my second invitation for you to believe and speak truth. Take a moment to *read aloud* the first four verses of Psalm 139 (printed above).

As a member of the *I'm Special Sisterhood*, your ascent out of the pit of an unmet longing begins by grasping the promise in those four verses like a rock-climber reaching for fingerholds. Reversing the destructive cycle of wrong thinking and wrong standing hangs on your willingness to push away the lies you've believed and pull yourself up into truth. Learning and declaring the lines in our Manifesto of Acceptance is like adding carabiners to your climbing harness. The first line of the Manifesto secures you to the overarching theme of Psalm 139:1–4.

God knows me.

Much easier to memorize than the four verses above, this three-word line has life-giving power when you speak it.

God knows me.

Say it loud enough for the sound to bounce off the walls of that pit you've been in and penetrate your heart.

God knows me.

The Bible tells the story of a woman who learned this simple truth. The woman at the well asked for living water and received far more than expected. She encountered the God who knew everything about her and discovered the joy of acceptance. I can't help but wonder if she grew to love Psalm 139 after she met Jesus. I grin imagining her visiting a newly established house church in her village, hearing the psalm read by another recent convert, and agreeing with its author from the depths of her soul. Join me on a journey back to the day of her discovery, as we imagine what her introduction to Jesus might have been like.

Running into Truth

Part of me secretly hopes you've never heard about the unusual encounter between Jesus and the woman at the well. Sadly, the familiar loses its wonder. Sadder still, a misunderstanding of the familiar confuses the truth. I had fallen into that rut by comparing the woman at the well to Hollywood starlets who jump from one marriage bed to the next. A preacher jolted me out of that pattern of wrong thinking when he confessed his own practice of misrepresenting the woman at the well. He explained to an arena full of people what I already knew but had somehow missed in the context of this woman's story. When Jesus walked the earth, a woman didn't have the right to divorce her husband. Only a man could casually dismiss his wife. The woman at the well's history of failed marriages had little to do with promiscuity and everything to do with rejection.

The woman had at least six reasons not to trust men when she arrived at the well and saw a man resting nearby. His clothing marked him as a Jew, which may have evoked an odd sense of relief. She lugged her water jar in the heat of the day to avoid running into the Samaritans from her village who knew her past. Knew her failure. Knew her shame. The woman had no reason to believe the Jewish stranger would know anything about her. Nor should he care to. After all, she was a Samaritan. And a woman. Jews didn't associate with her kind, and no pious Jew would speak with a woman alone. And yet the narrative in John 4:1–42 tells a different story. I encourage you to read it—even if you've heard it, read it, or studied it before. I hope by now you have a bookmark handy and aren't surprised when I send you to your Bible. Just don't forget to come back!

Most Jewish travelers between Jerusalem and Galilee went out of their way to avoid passing through Samaria. But not Jesus. He saw Samaria as a ripened field and its people as souls ready for harvest. So Jesus engaged the woman at the well in conversation. Her guard must have shot up at his request for a drink of water, because she responded by pointing out the obvious and challenging him with a question.

She said to Jesus, "You are a Jew, and I am a Samaritan woman. Why are you asking me for a drink?"

One of the things I love about Jesus is the way he responds to questions. Rather than answering, he often redirects the inquirer. He typically does this by asking a question of his own; but this time, he simply plants one, seeding the woman at the well with mysterious words that thirst for answers.

Jesus replied, "If you only knew the gift God has for you and who you are speaking to, you would ask me, and I would give you living water."

He asks her for a drink. She asks him why. He shifts to "what" (the gift God has for you) and "who" (the stranger speaking to you).

I picture the woman looking from Jesus to her jar and back at Jesus. With no understanding of why this Jewish man has chosen to request a drink from a Samaritan outcast, she raises another question, with her guard still up.

"But sir, you don't have a rope or a bucket," she said, "and this well is very deep. Where would you get this living water? And besides, do you think you're greater than our ancestor Jacob, who gave us this well? How can you offer better water than he and his sons and his animals enjoyed?"

Jesus doesn't interrupt when she points out his lack of water-drawing utensils. He doesn't object as she schools him on the depth, greatness, and history of the well. Nor does he answer a single one of her questions. Instead, Jesus offers to quench her thirst. Forever.

The "what" and "who" of Jesus drown out the "why" and "how" of the woman. Her guard slips, and she asks Jesus for his living water.

Let that sink in.

The woman came to the well in the heat of the day to shield herself from people. By accepting his offer, she could avoid this trek's routine reminder of her history with rejection. She wants water, but Jesus wants to quench a deeper thirst. He exposes her secrets and then covers her with the truth of who he is.

The Bible says the disciples appeared the very moment Jesus declared, "I am the Messiah!" They look shocked. The woman would have known that the disciples had caught Jesus breaking the rules of proper discourse at that moment, but were they also surprised by his declaration? They stood there stunned and speechless with the food they had purchased from the village. No one disturbed the awkward silence. The revelation hung in the air. Jesus claimed to be the Messiah!

Drink in the wonder.

Jesus revealed his identity—for the first time from his own lips—to free a rejected woman from the bonds of isolation. His declaration lead to breakthrough! A fresh, bubbling spring of living water gushed into the woman's soul, refreshing her spirit with the hope of eternal life.

Leaving her water jar beside the well, she ran back to her village with nothing to weigh her down.

No condemnation. No fear. No doubt.

The Bible says she told everyone, "Come and see a man who told me everything I ever did! Could he possibly be the Messiah?" She ran straight to the people who knew her past failures, but she felt only hope for her future.

No shame. No regret. No reservations.

The woman no longer needed the approval of others. Her thirst for acceptance had been satisfied. She had tasted living water.

I love happy endings! The conclusion of this story couldn't get any better. The Bible says,

> Many Samaritans from the village believed in Jesus because the woman had said, "He told me everything I ever did!" When they came out to see him, they begged him to stay in their village. So he stayed for two days, long enough for many more to hear his message and believe. Then they said to the woman, "Now we believe, not just because of what you told us, but because we have heard him ourselves. Now we know that he is indeed the Savior of the world."

This happy ending testifies to the overflowing spirit of the woman at the well, but she could only do what she could do. If the villagers hadn't accepted her invitation to come and see Jesus for themselves, the story would have concluded differently. I'm so glad they left their routines, engaged their minds, and opened their hearts to hear from Jesus. This is my prayer for you, sister. Even though your journey to discovering the joy of acceptance is just beginning, I'm already anticipating a happy ending. Your path to freedom may start with believing and speaking the first truth in our Manifesto: God knows me.

First Journal Prompt: Psalm 139:1–4

May I be frank with you? Simply reading this book won't satisfy your longing to belong. You may escape by reading stories like the one about the woman at the well, and you may gain insight from the instruction I present, but climbing out of the pit of rejection takes tenacity. The way up and out hangs on believing the truth (right thinking) and speaking it out loud (right standing). The tools to scale the pit are within your reach.

While I don't claim to have the formula to quench your thirst for acceptance, I know what gratifies mine. Daily pouring myself into the five-step method of journaling I introduced earlier sustains me better than ten 8-ounce glasses of water. Each time I open my Bible and record my thoughts, God meets me on the pages, where he teaches me truth and exposes each lie. He never ceases to equip me with right thinking. When I take the next step and declare what I've learned, God faithfully leads me into right standing.

I have found the place where I belong.

In the process of healing me from the sting of rejection, God convicted me of something that ultimately led to this book. If you and I believed—deep down, truly believed—every single word of Psalm 139, we would never suffer from chronic rejection. We would never entertain the lie that calls us unacceptable. We would know the truth of our tremendous worth and show the lie the door.

I invite you to accept the challenge to journal through Psalm 139. You'll find complete instructions at the back of this book on a page you can easily remove and paste to the front of your journal. I stand by my promise to guide you through the process until it becomes a comfortable routine. I've been following the look, list, learn, listen, and live formula for twenty years. I read God's Word and write down what it says, what it teaches, how it speaks to me, and how I'm going to respond to it. After filling more journals than I can count, I promise you this method works.

From this point forward, you will find a journaling prompt after each sketch. If I've done my job, you will see the correlation between the circumstances faced by the Bible character profiled and the verses you will read and write about.

The woman at the well carried an empty jar and lived an empty life—until she met Jesus. Based on what we know about her, rejection played a significant role in ruining more than her reputation. Her story, which aligns with Psalm 139:1–4, ends well because she learned the principle of the first line in our Manifesto of Acceptance: God knows me.

If you crave the security that comes from a rock-solid relationship, I invite you to meet the one who knows everything you've ever done and loves you madly anyhow. Will you complete our first journaling activity? I encourage you to drink from the first four verses of Psalm 139 and learn the truth of the first line of our Manifesto: God knows me. You may discover your true identity and—like the woman at the well—quench your thirst with living water.

Please bookmark this page and reach for your journal. I'll be waiting for you when you come back.

Leave the Lies like the Woman Left Her Jar

The woman at the well left her jar, ran to her village, and exclaimed, "Come and see a man who told me everything I ever did!" Why would someone with a dishonorable past broadcast her excitement at being exposed? The answer lies in a Greek dictionary. I'm no expert in ancient languages, but I became a fan of word studies upon learning the Old Testament was written in Hebrew and the New Testament in Greek. At times, curiosity begs me to look up certain words in their original language. I can't say for sure if my inquisitive nature or the Holy Spirit prompted me to hone in on the word "left" in the Biblical account of the woman at the well. The word appears twice in all of John 4. Hardly noteworthy. Until I learned the word doesn't mean what you might expect—in both instances.

I first noticed the unobtrusive word when I read that the woman *left* her jar and ran to the village to testify about her remarkable encounter. Jesus had just offered her living water, and the next thing you know, she's running off without her jar. Later, I found the word near the beginning of the chapter describing the way Jesus *left* Judea.

One commentary noted the Greek word used is "a very peculiar word for a simple departure." How curious. The commentary continues, "The verb [*aphiēmi*] is used when [*kataleipō*] might have been expected."[1] The "expected" word, *kataleipō,* means to leave behind, to depart from, to forsake or abandon. When Jesus left Judea and the woman left her jar, they didn't simply depart from a place or leave something behind. The verb translated as "left" in my Bible has a far deeper meaning. Do you see why word studies fascinate me?

The Greek word *aphiēmi* primarily means to send away, as in to yield up, to let go or let be, to disregard. The word *aphiēmi* defines Jesus's state of mind when he arrived in Samaria. It also hints at what no longer affected the woman when she burst into her village.

We'll explore the application of *aphiēmi* in Jesus's journey later. For now, let's consider why the woman left her jar at the well. Why did she *send away* the shame that bound her to lonely walks for water and *let go* of the labels that stuck to her like a branded past? Why did she *yield up* her empty excuses and *disregard* the opinions of the village folk? For the same reason the first disciples *left* their fishing nets. Yes! The exact Greek word, *aphiēmi,* describes how Peter and his brother Andrew responded when Jesus said, "Follow me." These two men left their livelihood and walked away from the security of the familiar.

Why hold onto past disappointments when you can embrace future possibilities? That question isn't meant to be rhetorical. I'm asking you to leave your water jar and fishing nets—the negative labels and unhealthy attachments that mask the real you—and begin a grand adventure of discovery. Once you sip the security of being fully known by God, you can't help but taste freedom. Quenching your thirst for acceptance flows from your willingness to agree with God about three things:

1. Who I am
2. Who he is
3. What I've done

If you were to draw a two-column table for each item above and write what you say on one side and what God says on the other, would the columns match? Would you even know what to write on God's side?

A gap often exists between knowing the truth and accepting it. Since we can't fully accept something we don't know, let's start with the facts.

You didn't create yourself.

While the world's stage has yet to draw the final curtain on the origins of life, overwhelming evidence casts an intelligent designer in the leading role. This book is based on the premise that God created you in his image, in which case agreeing with him about who you are, who he is, and what you've done may help you find your key to freedom.

Let's take a closer look at what God says about these three important matters.

Agreeing with God about Who I Am

I recently watched a video clip of Dr. Guy Winch, psychologist and author, giving a captivating TED Talk on emotional first aid.[2] He argues that good health demands that we tend to our emotions with the same diligent level of care we give our bodies. He tells a compelling story to illustrate our unhealthy tendencies. Here's a condensed snippet of Dr. Winch's full presentation:

> I once worked with this woman who after twenty years of marriage and an extremely ugly divorce was finally ready for her first date. She had met this guy online, and he seemed nice, he seemed successful, and most importantly, he seemed really into her.
>
> She bought a new dress, and they met at an upscale New York City bar for a drink. Ten minutes into the date, the man stands up and says, "I'm not interested," and walks out.
>
> The woman was so hurt she couldn't move. All she could do was call a friend. And here's what the friend said.
>
> "Well, what do you expect? You have big hips. You have nothing interesting to say. Why would a handsome, successful man like that ever go out with a loser like you?"

Shocking, right? That a friend can be so cruel.

But it would be much less shocking if I told you it wasn't the friend who said that. It's what the woman said to herself.

And that's something we all do, especially after a rejection. Our self-esteem is already hurting. Why would we want to go and damage it even further? We wouldn't make a physical injury worse on purpose. You wouldn't get a cut on your arm and decide, "Oh I know, I'm going to take a knife and see how much deeper I can make it."

Proverbs 18:21 says the tongue has the power of life and death. Yet we carelessly speak without thinking. We also think without thinking. In other words, we don't stop to taste the flavor of what our minds are chewing on. We give power to negative thoughts when we swallow them, hook, line, and sinker. We mustn't take the bait. It's tempting. I know. Especially when we're simply repeating what we hear. So what have you been hearing? What words ring in your head?

Whether criticism is shouted by a parent who thinks you never do anything right, a boss who always overlooks your best efforts, a spouse who can be difficult, or whether the self-condemnation is whispered over and over in your mind like a meme mocking you for not measuring up, the disparagement can easily shape what you believe about your identity.

In her book *Uninvited*, Lysa TerKeurst wrote, "Rejection isn't just an emotion we feel. It's a message that's sent to the core of who we are, causing us to believe lies about ourselves, others, and God."[3]

Why do we agree with that message?

I'm done. I hope you're done too. Let's commit to no longer allow insecurity or inadequacy or any other lie to define us. Let's use the power of the tongue to speak life, hope, and purpose.

Strong's concordance gives this word picture for the definition of *aphiēmi*: "to bid going away . . . of a husband divorcing his wife."

You and I don't have to stay married to a single lie about who we really are. We can partner with truth. We can declare: Lies, I bid you go away. This isn't a trial separation. I'm filing for divorce from you. Lies, you will no longer influence my mind. I choose to agree with God about who I am.

Want to know the best way to hear from God about who you are? Read his Word. It has a lot to say about you. For example, Deuteronomy 7:6 says, "For you are a holy people, who belong to the LORD your God. Of all the people on earth, the LORD your God has chosen you to be his own special treasure." And 1 Peter 2:9 calls you God's special possession. Obviously, God agrees with our secret signal. Do you remember learning it earlier? (It's American Sign Language for "I'm special.") By signing, "I'm special," you agree with God about your value. You align your thoughts with truth. You tell it like it is.

Declaring our Manifesto of Acceptance also brings you into alignment with truth. We're just getting started with learning the first of seven life-giving affirmations crafted to help you tell it like it is. Here comes another invitation to believe and speak truth. Declare the first affirmation aloud now.

God knows me.

Have you grasped the full meaning of being known by God? John Gill's *Exposition of the Whole Bible* describes it as

> particular, distinct, and complete; and is to be understood, not of his omniscience in general, so all men are known by him; but of his special knowledge, joined with affection, [approval], and care: and the meaning [of being known by God] is, that [you are] loved by him with an everlasting love.[4]

In other words, God would vigorously nod his head to hear you say, "To know me is to love me."

If you and I are going to agree with someone about who we are, shouldn't it be the one who knows us better than anyone?

Think about what you're thinking about yourself. Do the words bouncing around in your mind and rolling onto your tongue agree with what God says about you? The next time someone cuts you with words, please don't make the wound deeper. Agree with your Creator about who he created you to be, and discover—like the woman at the well—that knowing your true identity brings freedom.

Agreeing with God about Who He Is

A subtle tweak to a true statement can render it false. A slight variation from a rock-solid expression can rattle its foundation. A commonly repeated phrase that strays from truth advances a lie. I keep hearing one such subtly deceiving phrase. So much so that it's becoming a colloquialism. I've heard it spoken in unlikely circles—"godly" circles.

Please beware when you hear the phrase "my truth." I can have my own experience and perceive my own reality. I can live according to my own way and lead my own life. But no matter how real or lasting my experience may be, truth can't be defined by my terms if I'm living a lie.

I don't trust or want "my truth." I trust and want truth. Just. Plain. Truth.

What is truth? Pilate asked that question of Jesus when Truth was standing right in front of him. I spelled Truth with a capital T because Jesus called himself the way, the truth, and the life. He also said the truth will set you free.

I long for you to know Truth (Jesus) and be set free.

Once upon a time, telephones hung on walls. They kept us reined in with a curly cord that constantly twisted, rendering it shorter and shorter. The phone in my apartment during my college years had the longest curly cord money could buy. The day I learned the power of truth to change our perspective of life and death, I watched my roommate use every inch of that cord.

She stood in the kitchen when the voice at the other end of that wall-mounted phone broke the tragic news. Her oldest brother—who rejected the Christian faith every other member of her family had accepted, who moved all the way to Alaska to run from his parents' prayers, who lived life on the edge of danger as if immortal—had been killed in an avalanche. I will never adequately describe the sound erupting from her chest as she fell to the floor clinging to that corded handset. She bawled his name and screamed, "No, no, no."

I feared he was lost. Forever.

Apparently, the connection was disrupted, because the touch-tone Trimline phone—still pressed to her tear-stained face—rang.

"What?" Death fled the kitchen, and life raised my roommate to her feet.

"He did?"

I watched her listen, nod in silence, and hang up that old phone. I would learn of the tragic accident later. Her first words spoke of life, not death.

"Did you know Billy Graham was just in Alaska?"

I shook my head.

"My brother went forward to receive Christ."

Hope rushed through that little apartment. Truth transformed the atmosphere. When we agree with God for the very first time about who he is in Christ Jesus, we literally cross over from death to life. I love how The Message Bible presents Jesus's explanation of this in John 5:21–25:

But you haven't seen the half of it yet, for in the same way that the Father raises the dead and creates life, so does the Son. The Son gives life to anyone he chooses. . . .

"It's urgent that you listen carefully to this: Anyone here who believes what I am saying right now and aligns himself with the Father, who has in fact put me in charge, has at this very moment the real, lasting life and is no longer condemned to be an outsider. This person has taken a giant step from the world of the dead to the world of the living.

"It's urgent that you get this right: The time has arrived—I mean right now!—when dead men and women will hear the voice of the Son of God and, hear-ing, will come alive."

I feel the same sense of urgency. The time has arrived—I mean right now!—when the *I'm Special Sisterhood* stops believing lies about God and stops agreeing with lies attributed to God.

Jesus told the woman at the well, "You Samaritans know very little about the one you worship." I'm afraid the same could be said of many who worship him today.

In an effort to keep myself from believing lies about God, I often say a prayer inspired by Colossians 1:9–12: to be filled with the knowledge of God's will through all spiritual wisdom and understanding.

I urge you to do all you can to increase your knowledge of God. Knowing and agreeing with God's truth means accepting that his love for you is unfailing, his mercies unending, and his faithfulness enduring. God will never do or say anything to make you feel unloved, unworthy, or undesirable.

When you agree with God, your perspective changes—not only about who he is and who you are, but also about other absolutes. Align your truth with *the* truth, and any so-called truth will lose its power to influence your mind.

Agreeing with God about What I've Done

My parents taught me long ago that confession is all about agreeing with God. As a child who believed that God was always watching, agreeing with God kept me honest about who really broke Mom's crystal vase. Since God knew the truth, how could I deny it? Thankfully, my parents also taught me 1 John 1:9: "But if we confess our sins to him, he is faithful and just to forgive us our sins and to cleanse us from all wickedness."

The Greek word for "confess" in this verse is *homologeo*. This word means to say the same thing as another, to agree with; not to refuse, not to deny; to profess, to declare openly, speak out freely; to praise, celebrate.

Whether we feel free to openly declare the wrongs we've committed—let alone praise and celebrate in the aftermath—depends on whom we are agreeing with. Admitting to a failure or fault is much easier when I confess to someone who loves me unconditionally and keeps no record of wrongs. It also helps when that someone knows of my misdeeds before I confess them.

Prior to stopping for a drink in Samaria, Jesus knew the entire backstory concerning the sinful woman at the well. He knows as much about you and me. I promise you this: God already knows what you've done—whether you're responsible for a broken vase, a broken vow, or a broken life. And he loves you madly anyhow.

The message of "I know all your secrets and still love you" hit me with tremendous force as I journaled through Psalm 139:1–4 with the look, list, learn, listen, and live method I've been touting. I'm going to make a rare offer for you to peek at my entries associated with our first journaling activity. When I worked through these verses, I'd been reading from a different version than the one printed at the beginning of this chapter. Therefore, my List column may sound a little different than yours. Oddly, that's the one column that stays fairly consistent from person to person and from year to year. (Yes, I have on occasion revisited a past journal entry and marveled at how differently I see the Scriptures from my current outlook. God's Word is alive, and while he doesn't change, I certainly do.)

To begin my quiet time communing with God, I normally say a prayer similar to the one Eli taught Samuel in 1 Samuel 3:1–10: "Speak, LORD, your servant is listening."

After preparing myself to hear from God that day, I looked at these verses in my New International version of the Bible:

Psalm 139
¹ You have searched me, LORD,
 and you know me.
² You know when I sit and when I rise;
 you perceive my thoughts from afar.
³ You discern my going out and my lying down;
 you are familiar with all my ways.
⁴ Before a word is on my tongue
 you, LORD, know it completely.

In my List column, I wrote:

List

1. You have searched me, Lord (Yahweh, Jehovah, self-existing, eternal one), and you know me.
2. You know when I sit and rise. You know my faraway thoughts.
3. You know what I do and what I usually do, my habits.
4. Before I speak, you know my words.

I hesitate to share my Learn column. I can pick up the Bible and see something today that I didn't even notice the last time I read the same passage. God always has something distinct and relevant to say. I may need to learn a certain fact one day and an entirely different one the next day, or month, or year. When I examine the facts from Scripture and put my pen to the Learn column, the lessons jump off the page, depending on what I need in that season of my life. The journal entry you are about to read is what I needed to see.

God speaks to each of us individually. Your journal may look very different, and that would be wonderful proof that God knows you and knows what you need from him. In my Learn column, I wrote:

Learn

God has made a diligent study of me. Not a mere glance my way or a superficial assessment of me. He has read and researched and cross-referenced every page of me. God's knowledge of me is deep and lasting. He didn't cram for a test and then forget. He knows me like something that is ever before him. God doesn't have to stalk me or corner me or get in my face to keep track of my activities and thoughts. He simply knows the inner workings of my mind and sees what I do because he is God. At any given moment, he is already reading my mind. I don't have to know and verbalize my own thoughts for God to know what they are. He knows what I'm going to say before I do.

The Listen column has been my favorite step since I began this method of journaling in January 2000 (a New Year's resolution that actually stuck). Nothing competes with the thrill of hearing the voice of God. I listen with expectancy, and usually a clear thought will pop into my head in the form of a question—but only after I attentively look, list, and learn.

At this point, one question consumed my thoughts. I didn't know it would be the only one God would give me to ponder as I jotted it down in my Listen column.

> <u>Listen</u>
>
> Why does God's knowledge of me give me security?

The short query triggered an immediate response. I didn't wait for another question to come to mind. I began to write with urgency, filling the rest of the Listen column and every available line in the Live column. I only stopped writing when I ran out of room.

> <u>Live</u>
>
> Wow! I NEVER have to worry that you'll turn your back on me after some deep, dark secret is exposed. You really do know me better than I know myself, and you will NEVER leave me or forsake me. Nothing I could ever do or say or even think will ever surprise you. You have already made the decision through the sacrifice of your Son—your BELOVED Son—to love me forever, to cover everything I do, say, or even think that is displeasing or repugnant to you. I am absolutely secure in the

knowledge of your unfailing love for me because you won't change your mind about me. First of all, you're unchanging—period. But your thoughts for me will never change because you won't suddenly discover something new about me that changes your mind. You won't say, "Now that I know this about her, I don't love her anymore." You love me now and forever, no matter what. How could anyone ever be more secure in a relationship than I am with you? Thank you. Thank you for KNOWING ME, and knowing that will help me in my battle to feel accepted and significant and adequate and wanted. You really are a good and loving Father. I love you so much!

Drinking the living water Jesus offers is like consuming pure, hundred proof security. My past doesn't matter to the one who knows my true identity. He knows your past and identity, too, and he loves you. In fact, he thinks you are special—which reminds me of our secret signal. Now is as good a time as any to practice it.

Sign "I'm" by pointing to yourself midchest with the index finger of your right hand.

Sign "special" by holding out in front of you the finger you just used to point to yourself. With your fingerprint facing you as you point up, grab your right fingertip with the fingertips of your left hand, and pull straight up a couple inches.

Have you practiced the *I'm Special Sisterhood* secret signal in front of the mirror yet? I long to hear you say, "I'm special" to your beautiful reflection. Claiming your rightful place of belonging may hinge on seeing yourself through God's eyes. When he looks at you, he sees someone worth dying for.

A few pages back, I gave the Greek definition of the word often translated in our Bibles as "confess." The word *homologeo* appears in 1 John 4:15 below. Can you find it?

All who declare that Jesus is the Son of God have God living in them, and they live in God.

The King James Version actually translates *homologeo* as "confess," as do many modern translations, like this one from the Message:

Everyone who confesses that Jesus is God's Son participates continuously in an intimate relationship with God.

There's no greater confession you could make than to agree with God about his plan for your salvation. You can make that declaration right now with this simple prayer:

Father God,

I confess I'm a sinner.
I ask for your forgiveness.
I believe Jesus died for my sins.
I believe he rose from the dead.
I trust Jesus as my Savior.
I will follow him as my Lord.
Lead me into all truth, oh God.
Help me do your will.
I ask in Jesus's name.
Amen.

Experience the freedom God offers to all who worship him in spirit and in truth. Dive to a deeper level of trusting God, who knows your sins and failures intimately, and yet continues to love you unconditionally. Your commitment to journal through Psalm 139 will increase your knowledge of God, even as our first journaling activity focuses on his knowledge of you. If you skipped the activity earlier, I encourage you to do it now before moving on to the next story and declaration. I'll be waiting, even though I'm anxious to put the whole Manifesto in your mouth.

For now, we're off to a good start with one simple truth: God knows me.

Chapter Three

HE IS ALWAYS WITH ME

Psalm 139:5–8
⁵ You go before me and follow me.
You place your hand of blessing on my head.
⁶ Such knowledge is too wonderful for me,
too great for me to understand!
⁷ I can never escape from your Spirit!
I can never get away from your presence!
⁸ If I go up to heaven, you are there;
if I go down to the grave, you are there.

I love verse eight's echo, "You are there . . . you are there." Knowing I can count on God to always be there calms my fears. Since God is with me no matter where I go, I'm never alone, no matter where I am.

As you did with the first four verses of Psalm 139, please read verses 5–8 aloud.

I love the sound of the second line of the Manifesto. Saying this five-word phrase, which summarizes the truth of Psalm 139:5–8, fills me with peace.

He is always with me.

God's omnipresent nature permeates the universe. You may not be aware of his nearness, but God is closer than your heartbeat—even as he sits enthroned on high. God's supernatural ability to be in all places at all times means you couldn't get away from him even if you tried.

"If I go up to heaven, you are there; if I go down to the grave, you are there."

David's words remind me of God's words in Jeremiah 23:23–24:

> "Am I a God who is only close at hand?" says the LORD.
> "No, I am far away at the same time. Can anyone hide
> from me in a secret place? Am I not everywhere in all
> the heavens and earth?" says the LORD.

How does the thought of being hemmed in on all sides by the God of all creation make you feel? It depends on your perception of him, doesn't it? For David, knowledge of God's nearness was "too wonderful." David gratefully acknowledged the constant presence of the one he couldn't see.

In her book *Jesus Calling*, Sarah Young writes, "The curse of this age is overstimulation of the senses, which blocks out awareness of the unseen world. . . . The goal is to be aware of unseen things even as you live out your life in the visible world."[1]

The inability to see God doesn't make our newest declaration any less true.

He is always with me.

Long before David wrote Psalm 139, Joshua knew God went before him and followed him. Through forty years of wilderness wanderings, Joshua and all of Israel beheld God's glorious presence daily, revealed in a pillar of cloud by day and a pillar of fire by night. This tangible view of God surely carved Joshua's neuropathways with a deep impression of God's constant presence—a principle I want indelibly imprinted upon your mind by the time you reach the end of this book.

Please declare the second line of the Manifesto aloud now.

He is always with me.

Joshua's contact with the pillars of God's presence most likely discontinued on the plains of Moab, right around the time Moses died, and right before Israel reached the promised land. Joshua not only lost his mentor at this profound juncture; he also lost his tangible view of God. Joshua took up the mantle of leadership with no pillars to reveal God's presence and no mentor to remind of God's faithfulness.

Let your imagination wander all the way to the east side of the Jordan River, where Joshua received assurance through a beautiful promise echoed in our newest declaration.

He is always with me.

Never Alone

Doing the right thing didn't prevent Joshua from suffering the consequences of others' poor choices (Num. 13:30–31, 14:9). When he and Caleb returned from spying out the promised land with ten others, all twelve spies agreed the land was flowing with milk and honey. However, Joshua and Caleb alone believed God could be trusted. They demonstrated their faith by saying, "Let's go at once to take the land. We can certainly conquer it!"

The other ten gave a bad report, saying, "We can't go up against them! They are stronger than we are!" They fearfully declared they felt like grasshoppers compared to giants.

Joshua and Caleb stood firm, saying, "Do not rebel against the LORD, and don't be afraid of the people of the land. They are only helpless prey to us! They have no protection, but the LORD is with us! Don't be afraid of them!"

The Israelites chose cowardice and rebellion over courage and victory. Their tongues dripped with death as they discussed stoning Joshua and Caleb, but God intervened. I'm convinced the pain of abandonment—as cutting as the rocks that were never thrown— marked both ends of Joshua's wilderness wanderings. On the front end, the Israelites' rejection robbed Joshua of forty years in a land flowing with milk and honey. On the back end, Moses's death kept Joshua from continued reliance on his larger-than-life mentor.

According to Deuteronomy 34:10–12, "There has never been another prophet in Israel like Moses, whom the LORD knew face to face. . . . With mighty power, Moses performed terrifying acts in the sight of all Israel."

Moses wore some mighty big shoes. And Joshua had to fill those shoes prior to setting foot in the promised land.

I picture Joshua heading up from the plains of Moab to Mount Nebo, and climbing to the top of Pisgah Peak, across from Jericho. Standing in the very spot where God showed Moses the promised land, Joshua would be able to see Jericho's fortified walls. I imagine the sight would bring back memories of the decades-old report brought by his fellow spies, who feared the giants behind those walls more than they trusted God.

Like symptoms that flare up with a chronic illness, the chilling sense of abandonment rushes in at opportune times to freeze hope and fan fear. Joshua must have felt utterly alone as he mourned the death of Moses. His grief could have easily stirred up forty-year-old issues of abandonment. Joshua needed a reminder that God was still with him, even though the pillar of cloud by day and the pillar of fire by night no longer graced the camp.

Joshua's faith in God had certainly been refined and proven genuine, but I wonder about the depth of his faith in people. The cowardly community who rejected Joshua's admonition not to rebel against the Lord had done little to earn his trust. Sadly, Joshua also learned that even the best, most godly people couldn't always be trusted to do the right thing.

Do you know why Moses died before the Israelites crossed the Jordan River and fought the famous battle of Jericho?

God *kept* Moses from entering the promised land as a consequence of sin. As hard as it may be to believe, Moses—Joshua's larger-than-life mentor—failed his followers big time.

While grieving the death of his beloved sister, and under the stress of leading an entire nation through the wilderness, Moses was forced to deal with a life-threatening water shortage. Understandably, he went with his brother, Aaron, to the entrance of the Tabernacle and fell face down on the ground to pray. In response, God instructed Moses to speak to a designated rock while the people watched, and promised it would pour out plenty of water. Moses gathered the community around the rock, but instead of speaking to it, he struck it twice. God swiftly informed Moses of the consequences.

Though commended in the Bible as a prophet unlike any other in the history of Israel, Moses was kept from entering the promised land as a result of his disobedience. Even the best, most godly people sometimes do the wrong thing. Moses's grave error led to his death in the wilderness (Num. 20:1–13).

For Joshua, the circumstances surrounding the death of Moses must have been especially hard to stomach. An unbearably unfair form of abandonment, death causes irreversible desertion. No human being can keep a promise to never abandon us—not even people as heroic and holy as Moses. Only God can guarantee he will always be there for us.

Joshua endured rejection, betrayal, isolation, and abandonment. These painful experiences can wreak havoc on our ability to trust. But Joshua didn't place his trust in people. He placed his trust in God. From the early days of the exodus from Egypt, he learned of God's faithfulness by witnessing intimate conversations between Moses and God. What's more, Joshua remained inside the Tent of Meeting, where the Lord spoke to Moses face-to-face, even after Moses would return to the camp. Time spent alone with

God prepared Joshua to fill Moses's shoes. Joshua learned to tune his ears to hear the voice of God. Abandonment may well have marked both ends of Joshua's wilderness journey, but God helped him cancel any lingering fear of rejection, betrayal, and isolation shortly after Moses's death.

Turning the page from Deuteronomy 34 to Joshua 1 completes the epic storyline of Moses's leadership throughout the exodus and begins a new chapter for the people of Israel. God met Joshua at this profound juncture with a beautiful promise:

> No one will be able to stand against you as long as you live. For I will be with you as I was with Moses. I will not fail you or abandon you. . . . This is my command—be strong and courageous! Do not be afraid or discouraged. For the LORD your God is with you wherever you go. (Josh. 1:5, 9)

Forty years earlier, the ten spies responsible for spreading the bad report about the land had immediately died of a plague before the Lord. After four decades of wandering, every Israelite responsible for trading trust in God for cowardice had died in the wilderness. By the time Joshua reached the plains of Moab and surveyed the fortified city of Jericho, the nation that turned away from him had been replaced by a generation that looked up to him.

If you struggle with abandonment issues, be encouraged by Joshua's story. You, too, can discover the joy of acceptance through an intimate relationship with God. He is with you everywhere, always. Don't be afraid, sister. Your tongue has the power of life, so declare the truth of God's constant presence now.

He is always with me.

Second Journal Prompt: Psalm 139:5–8

No matter how isolated you feel, you are never alone. No matter your past rejections, God will never leave you. If your past is scarred by abandonment, cling to your loving, ever-present Father God, who promised to never leave you or forsake you.

God is always with you.

As you reach for your journal, take wrong thoughts captive by thinking about what you're thinking about and making sure your thoughts align with the truth.

Repeatedly responsible for robbing us of joy, abandonment is one of the biggest bandits of acceptance. It runs off with our need to belong and ransacks our sense of dignity. Emotions rubbed raw from a painful past make us vulnerable to believing lies about our current circumstances—lies that persist and persuade. We must believe and speak truth to cancel the negative effects of abandonment and rejection.

Journaling through Psalm 139:5–8 and meditating on its theme will help you learn the second line in our Manifesto of Acceptance.

He is always with me.

If you'd like a little more coaching through example, feel free to read on for now. I will be sharing more pages from my journal in the chapter ahead. If you're already comfortable with our five-step formula (look, list, learn, listen, and live), I encourage you to fetch your journal and set this moment aside to spend with God. While he is always with you, he especially enjoys focused time with you.

God Is with You to Bless You

I once gave my parents a blessing for Christmas. I resorted to giving a gift that money couldn't buy because I didn't have much money to buy a gift. In the years that followed, I would hear my dad repeat the story of the blessing he received that Christmas Day. He even used it as a sermon illustration—not just once to his own congregation, but over and over when he traveled and preached for other churches.

A blessing like the one I gave my parents—which I modeled after the one David mentions in Psalm 139—is transformative. No wonder David described the knowledge of God's hand of blessing upon his head as "too wonderful for me."

My parents' brightly wrapped package contained a hardback copy of *The Blessing* by Gary Smalley and John Trent. Their Christmas gift also included all five elements of the Hebrew blessing described in the book:

1. Meaningful touch
2. A spoken message
3. Attaching high value
4. Picturing a special future
5. An active commitment

Receiving a blessing is a big deal. In Genesis 27:30–34, Esau proved its value with his extreme reaction upon discovering his brother Jacob had stolen his blessing. The younger son masqueraded as the older and tricked their father into giving him the blessing meant for Esau. Jacob's deception caused his father to tremble uncontrollably and his brother to burst out with a loud and bitter cry, "Oh my father, what about me? Bless me, too!"

For more proof of a blessing's value, consider this testy exchange recorded in Mark's Gospel:

> One day some parents brought their children to Jesus so he could touch and bless them. But the disciples scolded the parents for bothering him.
>
> When Jesus saw what was happening, he was angry with his disciples. He said to them, "Let the children come to me. Don't stop them!"
>
> . . . Then he took the children in his arms and placed his hands on their heads and blessed them. (Mark 10:13–14a, 16)

Meaningful touch is the initial component of a traditional Hebrew blessing. In the verses above, Jesus placed his hands on the children's heads first, and then he blessed them. I'm convinced he didn't pull these little ones into a big group hug to issue a blanket blessing. I believe Jesus focused on each child, one by one, adhering to the same approach taken by the patriarchs when they blessed their children.

According to Psalm 139:5, your heavenly Father places his hand of blessing on your head. In other words, God singles you out and speaks into your heart to affirm your great worth and bright future. Even now, Father God is following through on his commitment to fulfill the blessing he has spoken over you. Perhaps you have sensed him prompting you to carry out the calls to action in this book. As you work your way through the verses of Psalm 139, you will receive all five elements of the Hebrew blessing. You tangibly affirm this blessing each time you grab your index finger to do the *I'm Special Sisterhood* secret signal and open your mouth to declare the Manifesto of Acceptance:

> God knows me.
> He is always with me.
> I am not invisible.
> I am wonderfully made.
> God's countless thoughts are for me.
> I have enemies, but . . .
> I can walk in victory.

We're just beginning to learn the Manifesto, but I couldn't resist spelling out the whole thing to illustrate how blessed we are. Are you beginning to understand why David's knowledge of God's hand of blessing was too wonderful for him?

God is with you now to bless you with a meaningful touch and a spoken message that attaches high value to you and pictures a special future for you. He is actively committed to ensuring that the words he has spoken over you are fulfilled.

As your comfort level with our journaling activities increases, your ability to discern the voice of God will also increase. You will hear him speak specific, personal words of blessing over you. His blessing has the power to heal you from the aching emptiness of abandonment and restore you completely—mind, body, and spirit.

Rejection Affects Our Minds

Abandonment can fester into rejection issues that trigger chronic emotional pain. Yesterday's rejection refuses to stay in the past, skewing perception of our current situation by affecting our thoughts and feelings—and ultimately our behavior. Consider as proof the way you react when you merely think of the person who abandoned you.

Healing from mental anguish hangs on conquering negative thought patterns with supernatural weapons. In the opening pages of this book, I called your tongue a God-given sword, a heaven-sent weapon, crafted to cut through lies and take thoughts captive. I encouraged you to use it to demolish strongholds by declaring the Manifesto. This battle plan to conquer wrong thinking and topple wrong standing comes from 2 Corinthians 10:3–5:

> For though we live in the world, we do not wage war as the world does. The weapons we fight with are not the weapons of the world. On the contrary, they have divine power to demolish strongholds. We demolish arguments and every pretension that sets itself up against the knowledge of God, and we take captive every thought to make it obedient to Christ. (NIV)

Taking our thoughts captive begins with thinking about what we're thinking about. Processing my thoughts on paper helps me diagnose the health and well-being of my mind. That's why I encourage journaling—especially by working through the five steps, as detailed in the appendix. Even as my journal entry for Psalm 139:5–8 exposed destructive self-talk, it also armed me with divinely powered weapons to stop the caustic cacophony.

In my List column, I summarized the facts—the literal meaning of Psalm 139:5–8.

<u>List</u>

5. You go before me and follow me. You place your hand of blessing on my head.
6. Knowing this is too wonderful and great to understand! It's lofty knowledge to attain.
7. I can never escape from your Spirit! I can never get away from your presence! Where can I go to flee from you?
8. If I go up to heaven, you are there. If I go down to the grave, you are there. If I make my bed in the depths, you are there.

The next journaling step offered no hint whatsoever that my mind was about to be laid open by a penetrating question from God. Here's what I wrote in my Learn column:

<u>Learn</u>

God steps out into my unknown future so I know the path ahead has already been cleared. Like those TV shows with police detectives going from room to room shouting, "Clear!" I don't have to be afraid of what's in front of me.

God also has my back. Nothing will sneak up behind me. God knows what's back there in my past or plotting to overtake me in the future.

God has given me the Hebrew blessing. It's amazing that he would speak over my life so personally and prophetically. Who am I that he would take such notice of every detail of my unfolding story? He lays his hand upon me because he wants me to succeed!

I couldn't get away from God even if I wanted to. He is everywhere always. His Spirit has a home in me, indwelling me because I invited Jesus into my heart. But even before he was in me, he was (and still is) all around me, not only in my highest moments of accomplishment, but also in my deepest pits of failure and my darkest times of sin. Not even death will separate us. God is always with me, and I am never alone.

I pray before tackling the fourth step—the one designed to help me hear the voice of God. In my flesh, I can read the verses, list what they say, and even jot down what lessons I learn from them. But the Listen column is different. I must quiet myself and patiently tune in to hear God's still, small voice. I try not to guess at what he is asking me, and I won't force a response. I wait until God chooses to speak. Sometimes, I have to move on with my day and leave that column blank because I don't hear anything. On this day with these verses, a couple of questions popped into my head right away. I wrote them in my Listen column.

Listen

Why do I fear the unknown when nothing about me or my circumstances are unknown to God?
What do I need to remember when I feel abandoned or alone?

I sensed God wanted to say something unexpected. So I reread the Learn column. My eyes lingered over this paragraph: *God has given me the Hebrew blessing. It's amazing that he would speak over my life so personally and prophetically. Who am I that he would take such notice of every detail of my unfolding story? He lays his hand upon me because he wants me to succeed!*

I shook my head and whispered, "You want me to succeed." Then this piercing question invaded my thoughts: *Why do you think my hand on you is heavy with expectations?*

I wrote it down in my journal as if asking myself the question.

Why do I think God's hand on me is heavy with expectations?

My throat knotted as God exposed the lie I believed about the weight of my responsibility to perform. As God revealed my unhealthy mindset, he issued a call to arms. By the time I reached the final journaling step, I was ready to wield my truth-talking tongue—peppered with the promise of God's hand of blessing—and demolish the argument that lied to me about God's expectations. In my Live column, I wrote:

Live

Dear God, why do I think that? Your hand is NOT heavy with expectations. You are so full of patience and grace—far more than I have for myself. I want to live in the freedom of knowing I delight you, just like my newborn granddaughter delights me. My daughter and I have no expectations whatsoever of that precious baby girl. I'm your girl. You are my God with a plan and purpose for my life, but you are also my daddy. You breathed life into me. Oh, Lord God, your hand of blessing is on my head! I know what that means and it's a LOT! To be blessed by you is far more than I deserve. Help me extend grace to myself and feel how secure but light your hand is upon me. I want the freedom of not being so hard on myself. I come under your mighty (but light) hand today and always. Amen.

God's hand of blessing eases the pressure to perform and secures an unconditional place of belonging. Will you allow him to touch your heart and heal your mind of the sting of abandonment? Though an entire nation abandoned Joshua, he chose to believe God's promise to be with him always. As he stood at the edge of the wilderness and faced the promised land, Joshua accepted the challenge to be strong and courageous.

What lies are you believing about God? Take wrong thoughts captive. Conquer them with divinely powered weapons. Begin to heal your mind by declaring the first two lines of the Manifesto of Acceptance.

God knows me.

He is always with me.

God has placed his hand of blessing on your head and will never leave you. He goes before you and follows you. He is actively committed to you and your future. Far from abandoned, you are chosen and accepted. As a matter of fact, sister, you are blessed.

Rejection Affects Our Bodies

My sixteenth birthday dawned with a rain-soaked sky. I refused to let the weather wash out my plans to head straight to the DMV from school. My mother recommended delaying my driving test for a brighter day, but I insisted.

"I want to get my license on my birthday."

I should've listened to my mom. The DMV official, clearly irritated at working in wet weather, barked at me to pull over a few short blocks from our starting point. I complied, pulling as far off the road as possible.

"Back up." He commanded.

The fogged up windows and piled up leaves shrouded the curb from view. I backed the car slowly and bumped the curb gently.

He failed me right then and there.

I later learned the infraction shouldn't have kept me from earning my license. (My girlfriend backed all the way up onto the curb and scored 95 out of 100.) I also learned the gloomy employee had a reputation for failing people without sufficient cause—a small consolation for not getting my license on my birthday.

After the sun came out, I returned to the DMV, only to have the same reviewer approach my car. He looked every bit as gloomy in the sunshine. The sight of that man clutching his clipboard smacked me with the agony of failure. My heart pounded. My palms dampened. My throat tightened. I wanted to object but couldn't speak. He grabbed my paperwork, looked it over, and shoved it toward me without meeting my eyes.

"I can't ride with you a second time." He withdrew and called over his shoulder. "I'll send someone else out."

To say relief flooded my soul would be an understatement. My body physically reacted with such force it's a good thing I was all buckled in. The jolly man who took me out for round two turned out to be the reviewer who had given my friend a 95. He gave me a perfect score.

Painful memories plague more than our minds. Dr. Guy Winch, from the previously mentioned TED Talk, also published an article that cites research indicating rejection causes actual neurological pain.[2] In fact, study participants who received Tylenol before recalling a painful rejection reported significantly less emotional pain than subjects who took a sugar pill. I should've taken Tylenol before going back to the DMV!

Analgesic drugs reduce the pain of rejection because when you and I experience rejection, the same areas of the brain become activated as when we experience physical pain.[3] However, physical pain stays in the past. Emotional pain doesn't. You and I can recount sports injuries or thirty-six-hour labor-and-delivery stories all day and never feel actual physical pain. Not so with rejection. Dr. Winch explains that recalling a time you suffered a painful rejection will flood your brain with many of the same feelings you had at the time, and reliving those memories will cause emotional pain all over again.

Many years after my sixteenth birthday, I discovered the cure for recurring emotional pain. This cure is much more powerful than aspirin or Tylenol. In her book *Uninvited*, Lysa TerKeurst writes, "Acceptance is like an antibiotic that prevents past rejections from turning into present-day infections."[4] I love that! Acceptance trumps analgesics as the antidote for abandonment. Better yet, you don't need a prescription for it, and you don't need a person to administer it. Swallow this truth whole now, my friend.

You don't have to wait for someone to accept you to be healed from the sting of past rejections. You can claim your place of belonging right now. Your tongue has the power of life and death. Restore health to your body and soul by believing and speaking truth. Knowing and declaring Psalm 139 as summarized in the Manifesto of Acceptance will inoculate you against toxic lies about your worth and identity.

God knows me.

He is always with me.

Whenever recalling a past rejection makes your heart pound, palms dampen, or throat tighten, remember that God is with you to bless you. He accepts you just the way you are.

Rejection Affects Our Spirits

The cheerleaders at my high school recognized one student during the fourth quarter of every football game by awarding the Spirit Stick for above-and-beyond support. The honored recipient took home the stick (a wooden relay baton), marked it in some indelible fashion, and returned it at the start of the next game. I won the Spirit Stick at an especially exciting game my sophomore year. I had laryngitis the next day—proof of a praiseworthy spirit, which my school measured in vocal and otherwise demonstrative loyalty to its football team.

Wearing school colors and chanting team cheers invites a spirit of belonging. Rejection summons an altogether different spirit—one that robs us of belonging. The author of Psalm 139 was well acquainted with the havoc this thief inflicted on Israel's first king. David entered into Saul's service to relieve the torment perpetrated by an evil spirit allied with rejection.

I want to pause before this difficult lesson to encourage you with the hope we have since Jesus satisfied the wrath of God. The circumstances that brought David to serve Saul occurred under the old covenant. New covenant believers have been made right with God through the sacrificial death of Jesus Christ on the cross. All who receive the gift of eternal life by faith in Jesus have been reconciled, justified, and redeemed. Jesus ushered in a standard of grace, mercy, and love. Sadly, Saul was held to a different standard. Since he rejected the word of the Lord, the Lord rejected him as king over Israel, which brings me back to the spirit of rejection and how David responded to its manifestation. You can find the account in 1 Samuel 16:14–23.

Soon after the Spirit of the Lord departed from Saul, an evil spirit arrived. The tragic story of Saul's demonic oppression begins with Saul's attendants telling him, "See, an evil spirit from God is tormenting you. Let our lord command his servants here to search for someone who can play the lyre. He will play when the evil spirit from God comes on you, and you will feel better."

I would understand if you questioned the idea of an evil spirit coming from God, but 1 Samuel 16 leaves no doubt.

Saul agrees to his servants' plan, and one of them tells him about David.

The servant said, "I have seen a son of Jesse of Bethlehem who knows how to play the lyre. He is a brave man and a warrior. He speaks well and is a fine-looking man. And the LORD is with him."

Saul sent messengers to Jesse, who responded by loading up a donkey and sending his youngest son to Saul. David entered Saul's service as one of his armor bearers, and Saul took an instant liking to him.

The last verse in this tragic story says, "Whenever the spirit from God came on Saul, David would take up his lyre and play. Then relief would come to Saul; he would feel better, and the evil spirit would leave him."

Saul's attendants could see evidence of the evil spirit torment-ing Saul. David clearly recognized the manifestation of the evil spirit too. No one directed him to pick up his lyre and play. He knew when to do it. David's music not only soothed Saul's spirit; it also caused the evil spirit to leave. Unfortunately, Saul's unbridled reaction to rejection beckoned the tormentor's return soon after young David defeated Goliath, the Philistine giant who terrified Saul and the entire Israelite army.

The rejection came in the form of a song sung by the women from the towns of Israel. As the victorious army led by King Saul marched past on its way home in 1 Samuel 18:6–12, the women danced for joy, played tambourines, and sang, "Saul has killed his thousands, and David his ten thousands!"

Saul didn't care for their song in the least. Insecure in his role as king and jealous of David's popularity, Saul allowed rejection to invade his thoughts and dictate his behavior. Saul's negative mindset opened him up to immediate and devastating consequences. Overwhelmed by a tormenting spirit, Saul began to rave like a madman.

I can relate to Saul's ranting and raving in response to rejection. I found myself in a position where I felt neither appreciated nor significant. My dear husband listened to me complain about it daily. My broken spirit argued within me that either those who devalued me were despicable or they were right. The longer they treated me with disregard, the more the spirit of rejection tormented me.

Let me pause again here to clarify the implications of using the word "spirit." I'm not suggesting a demon lurks behind every instance of rejection in your life or mine. But I want you to be aware of and open to the possibility. The emotional pain that troubles your mind and plagues your body also pierces your spirit, which opens you up to demonic attack. However, Christians have been given authority in Jesus's name to overcome all the power of the enemy and his demons. When you resist the devil, he will flee from you. If spiritual forces of evil are at work in your circumstances, know that Jesus himself promised nothing will harm you if you trust in him.

If your struggle has less to do with spiritual warfare and more to do with a self-deprecating battle confined to your mind, you still need to arm yourself with the unconventional weapons I mentioned previously. Winning the battle—whether you're fighting an evil spirit or a negative mindset—hangs on believing and speaking the truth.

What began as complaining to my husband about the people who rejected me could easily have escalated into a stronghold of bitterness. Thankfully, knowledge of Scripture and my husband's encouragement empowered me to renounce the lie that I was insignificant and worthless. I've learned that grumbling usually originates from thoughts that need to be captured. When I stop and think about what I'm thinking about, I'm far less inclined to turn into a raving lunatic. When I open my mouth and declare how blessed and loved I am by God, I'm much more likely to be in good spirits. Renouncing the lies and canceling their negative effects with Scripture is a winning strategy. I'll save the raving for an exciting football game.

Truth Heals Us Completely—Mind, Body, and Spirit
A verse from Psalm 139 says, "I can never escape from your Spirit! I can never get away from your presence!" The ever-present Holy Spirit played a huge role in my victory over the spirit of rejection. More than anything, the Holy Spirit gave me the courage to stand firm in my true identity.

God knows me.

He is always with me.

His Spirit does *not* make me timid but, rather, gives me power. Conversely, demonic spirits *do* try to frighten us. They also try to rob us of everything the Spirit gives. If we let them get away with deceiving us into relinquishing the power that rightfully belongs to us, we fall prey to fear. Timidity is a convincing liar. But remember, Jesus gave us authority in his name to overcome all the power of the enemy and his demons.

God doesn't give us a spirit of fear, but the enemy does. Fear often manifests when we're alone. That's why Satan tries to convince us that we've been abandoned. But Satan is a liar.

God never has and never will abandon his children. From his ancient promises spoken through Old Testament prophets to Jesus's words revealed to New Testament apostles, biblical assurances of God's constant presence abound. These promises speak of God's nearness as well as constancy. God doesn't merely glance your way from some high and lofty throne. He comforts you in times of trouble. He shelters you from evil. He walks with you through the darkest valley.

God is by definition omnipresent. If he is everywhere always, he *must* be with you where you are. Wherever you are. Always. God also *chooses* to be with you. He actually compared himself to a nursing mother. The next time you see someone cuddling a baby, think of the words God spoke through the prophet Isaiah:

> Can a mother forget the baby at her breast and have no compassion on the child she has borne? Though she may forget, I will not forget you! See, I have engraved you on the palms of my hands. (Isa. 49:15–16 NIV)

Let that soak in.

You may feel alone. But you are never alone. Even if your mother or father abandoned you, their actions can't erase the fact that God carved a reminder of you on his hands. A parent, husband, friend, or employer may have rejected you, but that doesn't brand you as being unwanted or unacceptable. If you've been abandoned, I urge you to accept the fact that God will never leave you.

He is with you now to heal you.

God's constant, nurturing presence remedies the residual pain caused by past abandonment. The power of God's love can cure rejection issues affecting your mind, body, and spirit. Begin the healing process right now by easing into the arms of God and tracing the imprint of you on his hands. Rest in the knowledge of your incredible worth, sister. God will never forget or abandon you. You belong in his loving arms.

If you skipped journaling through Psalm 139:5–8, I encourage you to do it now before moving on to the Psalm's next four verses and the third line from the Manifesto of Acceptance. Processing your thoughts on paper may help you diagnose the health and well-being of your mind.

Before picking up that journal, why not practice the *I'm Special Sisterhood* secret signal. As you reach for your right index finger with your left hand, picture God's hand of blessing on your head. And as you pull up on that finger and say, "I'm special," listen for God to attach high value to you and picture a special future for you—even if such knowledge is too wonderful for you.

You are special. That's a fact.

Chapter Four

I AM NOT INVISIBLE

Psalm 139:9–12

⁹ If I ride the wings of the morning,
if I dwell by the farthest oceans,
¹⁰ even there your hand will guide me,
and your strength will support me.
¹¹ I could ask the darkness to hide me
and the light around me to become night—
¹² but even in darkness I cannot hide from you.
To you the night shines as bright as day.
Darkness and light are the same to you.

The tongue has the power of life and death, and when the Word of God is on your tongue, you speak life. If you haven't already done so, please read Psalm 139:9–12 aloud.

I love this promise! Whenever people shove me into the shadows with their disregard (whether intentional or not), I'm tempted to take a negative tone. The promise in verses 9–12 helps me reign in destructive thoughts before they reach my tongue. I can shine light on foul attempts by darkness to snuff life out of my words. Knowing the night shines as bright as the day to God matters to me. It speaks tenderly into my lonely spaces where black clouds barrel in, unwelcome and unannounced, shrouding even the sunniest disposition. Perhaps that's why I declare the third line of the Manifesto more than any of the others.

I am not invisible.

As little ones, both my children incessantly called out. "Watch me, Momma. Watch me!" I'm convinced we were born with a need to be seen. One of God's names is El Roi, which means the God who sees. The promise in Psalm 139:9–12 testifies to the faithfulness of El Roi. He sees us in the piercing brightness of morning, and he sees us just as clearly in the dense darkness of night.

I am not invisible.

In my former role as a communications specialist, I attended a conference for first responders in law enforcement, health care, and education on the horrors of sex trafficking. I interviewed women rescued from prostitution. The women came from diverse socioeconomic, educational, and ethnic backgrounds, and each had her own heartbreaking story. Each had her own experience of neglect or abuse. However, they all shared at least one thing in common: they had been swallowed whole by darkness. Some of these precious, broken women had spent so long in the shadows that they had reached the point of no longer *wanting* to be seen.

Evil takes advantage of invisibility. But I am not invisible.

The Bible chronicles the brave actions of a prostitute named Rahab. Her story, found in the second and sixth chapters of Joshua, astounds me because she cared about saving her entire family. Though admittedly limited, my exposure to the world of sex trafficking has taught me that most women caught up in prostitution don't have healthy relationships with their families—especially their fathers.

I wonder why Rahab begged the Israelite spies to spare her family's lives when Joshua's army attacked Jericho.

I wonder how she summoned the courage to lie to the earthly king of Jericho while trusting the unseen, heavenly King.

I wonder.

Hope Hangs in the Window

I didn't intentionally choose a sequel from Joshua to illustrate the next line in the Manifesto of Acceptance. I simply closed my eyes and pondered whose story best aligns with the declaration "I am not invisible." Instantly, I pictured a scarlet rope hanging against a rock wall in Jericho.

Rahab's rescue relied on the visibility of a single scarlet rope. Her escape from a life of prostitution began when two Israelite spies descended from her window on that bright red rope. They had secretly been sent by Joshua himself to scout out the land around Jericho. Somehow his covert strategy was uncovered and reported to the king of Jericho, who learned the spies had entered Rahab's house and sent orders for her to hand them over.

Rahab's heart must have pounded when she lied in reply. She had hidden the spies under bundles of flax on her roof, but said, "Yes, the men were here earlier, but I didn't know where they were from. They left the town at dusk, as the gates were about to close. I don't know where they went. If you hurry, you can probably catch up with them" (Josh. 2:4–5).

Her deception worked. The king's men embarked on a vain mission while Joshua's spies nestled under bundles of flax within the very walls that would soon come tumbling down. To Rahab, the "giants" in her fortified city were like grasshoppers compared to the God of Israel. She knew about the miraculous Red Sea crossing. She knew Joshua had overpowered the two kings east of the Jordan River. She knew his army left no survivors. But how did she know to credit God for Israel's triumphs?

"I know the LORD has given you this land," she told the spies. "No one has the courage to fight after hearing such things [about Israel's triumphs]. For the LORD your God is the supreme God of the heavens above and the earth below" (Josh. 2:9, 11).

Rahab grew up in a pagan culture that didn't worship God or even believe in the existence of a singular Supreme Being. So how, when, and where did she learn about God? Did she watch the sunrise and wonder who made it appear? Did she look up at the stars and wonder who created them? Did she see God's invisible qualities through the things he made?

David bore witness to this possibility in Psalm 19:1–2:

The heavens proclaim the glory of God.
    The skies display his craftsmanship.
Day after day they continue to speak;
    night after night they make him known.

Apparently, Rahab didn't have a husband to take care of her financial needs, let alone her emotional needs. A woman with other means of support wouldn't normally choose prostitution as a revenue stream. Rahab needed a real-life rescuer, and she knew it. But how did she know the "supreme God of the heavens above and the earth below" would deliver her? How did she summon the strength to commit treason against her earthly king to align with an enemy army? How does a woman with no knowledge of God find the faith to trust him with her life?

The answer? Revelation.

Whether God silently revealed himself to Rahab through creation or spoke decisively to her through the miracle of the Red Sea crossing, Rahab learned the secret to seeing the unseen God. She also saw the probability of rescue. The clue to her clear view surfaced in the request she made to the spies after lying to the king's men. She returned to the hideout on the roof and said to Joshua's spies, "Now swear to me by the LORD that you will be kind to me and my family since I have helped you. Give me some guarantee that when Jericho is conquered, you will let me live, along with my

father and mother, my brothers and sisters, and all their families"
(Josh. 2:12–13).

Not one of the sexually trafficked women I interviewed at the
conference for first responders had a healthy relationship with her
dad. In fact, most had been runaways. Why would a woman who
experienced the trauma of running away from home show kindness to the people whose actions caused her to flee? I don't know
Rahab's family history, but I can't begin to picture her taking a day
off from selling herself to invite her father and mother, brothers
and sisters, and all their families over for dinner. Can you?

Before interacting with the rescued women who—as victims
of sex trafficking—once shared Rahab's ancient vocation, I might
not have noticed the unusual nature of Rahab's request. Her desire
to save her family from Jericho's destruction proved her willingness to let go of any bitter memories she may have had about
her upbringing. For Rahab, moving forward into the promised
land wasn't about possessing a land filled with milk and honey.
She already lived there. For her, receiving her inheritance meant
trusting God would guide and support her, whether she rode the
highest wings of morning or sank to the deepest depths of darkness.

Rahab knew she was not invisible to God. She believed he saw
through the shadows of her pagan culture, she trusted he saw past
her sinful lifestyle, and she risked her life to hide the spies who
represented the God she couldn't hide from.

I honestly don't know if Rahab was estranged from her family.
I don't know if abuse or neglect initiated her life of prostitution.
I don't know if she was a runaway like the women I interviewed
at that conference. But here's what I do know: holding onto the
people who hurt us requires letting go of the hurtful things they've
done to us. You and I can't live in freedom if we are bound by bitterness or unforgiveness.

If misplaced trust, broken relationships, or violation have driven you into the shadows, I hope Rahab's example draws you into the light. God sees you and the wrongs that have been done to you. He is a God of justice and mercy. Just look at what he did for Rahab. Ask him to make your rescue route as plain as a bright red rope. You are seen, sister. Believe and speak it for yourself.

I am not invisible.

Third Journal Prompt: Psalm 139:9–12

We have arrived at our third journal prompt. I wish I could walk alongside you and hear your thoughts on journaling like I did recently with a friend. She initially balked at my invitation to journal, which makes me sensitive to the possibility of your reluctance. I don't want my zeal for journaling to turn you off or chase you away. I know how intimidating an uncharted, blank page can be. At the same time, I believe with all my heart your journal journey will reveal hidden treasures. This activity is your road map to guide your discovery of acceptance.

My girlfriend's initial hesitation didn't stem from trivializing the transformative power of journaling. In her youth, she poured her heart into private journals and thoroughly enjoyed processing her thoughts and emotions—until her mother found and read them. No amount of well intentions could repair the damage of privacy lost. My friend vowed to never again expose her feelings on paper. Yet receiving my invitation to journal through Psalm 139 prompted her to rekindle her passion. She lives in a home of her own now with well-established boundaries and no reason to fear invasions of her privacy. Plus, she has access to a locking desk drawer.

If you're a veteran at keeping a journal, I hope you have adapted well to our five-step formula. If you've never journaled or gave it a stab and didn't like it, I encourage you to reconsider. If you've been painfully exposed through your vulnerability in the past, I beg you not to succumb to the power of fear. Climbing out of a pit of an unmet longing is much more difficult in the dark. I believe journaling through Psalm 139 will help light the way. I'm honored to be your guide.

You have reached the point of going solo with our five-step formula to study Scripture. Before approaching our next set of verses, you may want to revisit the instructions in the appendix or review excerpts from my journal in the previous two chapters. I'm confident that by now you will have no trouble with the Look, List, and Learn columns. If you don't feel ready to tackle the Listen column, please take time to inquire of God anyway.

Be still and be patient.

I believe God has something to say to you—something personal. Even if you think he has never spoken to you before, I believe you can hear and recognize his voice. Review the Learn column while asking God how to apply the lessons to your life. Tell him you want to please and obey him.

Be expectant and be flexible.

The voice of God probably won't boom with thunder from heaven. It's more likely to enter your mind like the sound of your own thoughts. Whether that whisper sounds familiar or not, hang on to what you hear. Ask God to quiet the other voices in your head so you can hear from him. Depending on your family background and experiences with authority figures, you may expect God to sound like a condescending father or Jericho's demanding king. The Bible tells us that God revealed himself to Rahab through his mighty power on behalf of Israel and through his loving acceptance of her—no matter her pagan culture, failed upbringing, or sinful lifestyle. When you seek God, he will never sound condescending nor demanding. He responds with love. Always.

Be discerning and be alert.

Write only those questions in the Listen column that a loving father or shielding king would ask. A loving father never tears down his child with condemnation. A shielding king never manipulates his servant with shame. Listen for gentle correction and helpful guidance.

Mark this page, and take the time to complete your journaling activity before continuing with the next section of this chapter. Even now, you are not invisible to your Heavenly Father. You hold the gaze of the King of kings, and his eyes are filled with love.

The Principle of Reciprocal Relatedness

Two-year-old Lily was all buckled into her car seat and securely riding in the back on the passenger's side of her grandmother's car when she suddenly disappeared.

"Can you see me, Grammie?" She called out to my girlfriend, who was driving. "I can't see you. Can you see me?"

Grammie glanced over her shoulder at her granddaughter and chuckled. Lily's pudgy little fingers covered her eyes.

"Yes. I can see you, Lily."

"I can't see you, and you can't see me." The preschooler contended.

"Where's Lily?" Grammie asked, playing along. "Where did she go?"

Lily raised her dimpled hands. "Here I am!"

Researchers have studied this behavior, calling it the principle of reciprocal relatedness—a fancy way of saying that perception and communication must flow both ways.[1] The findings were published in the *Journal of Cognition and Development* and aptly titled, "'Not See, Not Hear, Not Speak': Preschoolers Think They Cannot Perceive or Address Others without Reciprocity."

This opens up a whole new realm of adventure when playing peekaboo. Now that I know about this back-and-forth reciprocity thing, I'll pull the blanket, book, or other blinder away from my ears and mouth as well as my eyes before cooing the words "peeka-boo." Otherwise, my little playmate may not see, hear, or speak to me. I prefer a mutually shared peekaboo experience.

I wonder what would happen if this study extended beyond the natural realm. I'm convinced a huge sampling of grown-ups would respond like preschoolers (myself included). The principle of reciprocal relatedness with God might say, "If I can't see God's eyes, ears, or mouth, then he can't see, hear, or speak to me." We must sound like children asking God to play peekaboo. Thankfully, he is a patient and loving Father who does not judge it impossible to relate to us—even if we struggle with relating to him.

David knew communication with God flows both ways. His psalms teach us not only that God knows what we're going to say before we say it, but also that God bends down, listens, and answers as we pray. You and I can't see God, but that doesn't mean communication can't flow both ways. He looks upon us, hears our prayers, and speaks clearly to us.

Rahab grew up in a culture that didn't acknowledge God. However, her trust in the unseen God of Israel ran deeper than her fear of the authority figures she could lay her eyes on. Rahab's courage in lying to her king about hiding Joshua's spies indicates that she didn't insist on reciprocal engagement. She demonstrated a remarkable ability to embrace an invisible God. If Rahab was anything like the women I met who were rescued out of prosti-tution, then her request to save her father, mother, and all of her family took more than courage. She let go of her past but held onto her family. As I consider what could've motivated her to do this, I can't help but think of the Greek word describing how the woman at the well left her jar. The Old Testament was written in Hebrew, so you won't find this word in the biblical account of Rahab. When I first defined *aphiēmi* back in Chapter Two, I contrasted it with another Greek word translated as "to leave behind, to depart from, to forsake or abandon." Rahab didn't simply leave her past behind. She sent away her experience in Jericho and disregarded its effect on her. She divorced herself of its painful memories. Isn't this how the woman at the well left her jar?

In Chapter Two, I promised to explore why *aphiēmi* was used to describe how Jesus left Judea before arriving in Samaria, where he met the woman at the well. Jesus didn't simply depart from Judea. Instead, he disregarded the condemnation of the Pharisees who had heard of his growing ministry, and he entered Samaria with his thoughts unencumbered by the Pharisees' loathing. In this context, *aphiēmi* could well have been translated with a different English word. Rather than "So he *left* Judea," John 4:3 could have gone the way of Matthew 6:12: "[F]orgive us our sins, as we have forgiven those who sin against us." Because "forgive" appears in the original Greek as *aphiēmi*, John 4:3 could be interpreted this way: "So [Jesus] *forgave* Judea and returned to Galilee."

Rahab's actions appear to communicate the same mindset. She forgave Jericho, she forgave her family, and she forgave the men who used her for sexual pleasure. To clarify, Rahab's departure from Jericho isn't detailed in Scriptures, let alone spelled out with the word *aphiēmi*. Yet her actions show that her life of prostitution no longer exercised an influence on her mind. Her desire to save her parents, their children, and their grandchildren proves she valued familial relationships.

Rahab's legacy never would've grown from a bitter root. The first chapter of Matthew traces Jesus's roots all the way back to Abraham. Only five women are mentioned in his lineage. Rahab received the high honor of being one of them. The branches of her family tree convince me she extended forgiveness. Though referred to as a prostitute hundreds of years after Jericho's fall, Rahab is commended in Hebrews 11:31 and James 2:25 for her faith. Her legacy proves that even in darkness, we can't hide from God. To him, the night shines as bright as day.

Forgiveness Is Often Misunderstood

A visiting missionary told me about an observation she received from a young man who lived in the Third World country where she served.

"You Westerners bring your prayer requests to God like this," he said as he cupped his hands and held them out, ready to receive whatever might drop into them. "But we take them to God like this." He inverted his hands, unafraid of spilling what they held. He then flicked his fingers and thrust his palms downward—just to make sure they were empty. This action beautifully represents what the Bible teaches about forgiveness.

What if we reacted like the young man with the empty hands each time rejection stings us? What if we flung the pain of abandonment completely out of our hearts and minds? If we could grasp the true meaning of biblical forgiveness, we would be far less inclined to hold onto painful memories and far better equipped to respond to rejection in a healthy manner.

Misunderstanding the meaning of forgiveness can deceive us into wrong thinking and wrong standing. On the one hand, we may operate out of the belief that certain offenses should never be forgiven. Let's face it—some people don't deserve forgiveness, let alone ask for it. On the other hand, we may think God commands us to immediately and completely excuse our offender.

As one who leaned heavily to the "thou shalt forgive or else" side, I set myself up for repeated rejection. I didn't want to fall into a bitterness trap by refusing to forgive, but I became easy prey to maltreatment through my willingness to excuse inexcusable offenses. Nowhere in the definition of *aphiēmi* will you find the word "excuse." That's not true forgiveness, so don't believe for a minute that forgiving someone implies the wrongs committed were OK. One of my pet peeves is when I auto-respond to "I'm sorry" with "It's OK." No. It's not always OK. We may be able to work through the wrongdoing and restore the relationship, but this doesn't happen automatically. God is merciful, but he is also just. He does not excuse a single offense. Jesus had to die to pay the penalty for sin. Forgiving doesn't give a free pass for wrongdoing. Instead, forgiving releases you from the role as judge and drops the responsibility into God's hands. When you forgive someone, you

1. Renounce your right to judge or seek revenge
2. Release your offender to God

Forgiving frees you from dwelling on the negative effects of the offender's wrongdoing. This freedom helps ease the pain caused by recalling the wrongs you suffered. And speaking of memories, please erase this popular phrase from your mind for good: forgive and forget. You may never forget, and that's OK. Remembering past offenses can teach us valuable lessons. The idea that we are supposed to forgive and forget is a myth. God is the one who forgives wickedness and forgets sin. We are not God. He doesn't expect us to forgive exactly like he does.

Another misunderstanding about true forgiveness comes from the idea that we must confront the offender in order to forgive. According to the original Greek language, forgiving an offense *sends away* the negative effects and *disregards* the offender. You can forgive someone without ever seeing or speaking to that person again. You may want to write a letter to express your feelings, but you may choose to never send it. That's OK. Confronting the offender is only necessary if you desire reconciliation.

Reconciling with the offender isn't a requirement of biblical forgiveness. In fact, the definition of *aphiēmi* includes, "to bid going away or depart, of a husband divorcing his wife." That sounds like the opposite of reconciliation to me. If you don't want the offender in your life, you don't have to seek reconciliation. If reconciliation has been a stumbling block to forgiveness, then let me roll it away. Making up and moving forward takes two people willing to right wrongs and make amends. Forgiveness takes only one, which also means forgiveness does not require an apology.

I find it much easier to forgive someone who apologizes. My husband and I attended a marriage conference a few years after Scott was born. We learned a five-step apology that we brought home to Scott and his big sister, Sarah. My daughter was old enough to learn it, but my three-year-old son had a harder time with the concept of apologizing appropriately. We rehearsed it repeatedly:

1. I'm sorry.
2. I was wrong.
3. I won't do it again.
4. Will you forgive me?
5. Can we start over?

This wonderful formula walked my children through the entire forgiveness process, which in their case included reconciliation. I taught them that you're not truly sorry if you don't acknowledge wrongdoing and promise to discontinue the wrong behavior. They learned the offender was responsible for parts one, two, and three of the five-step apology. However, the person who had been harmed controlled what happened from then on. An apology does not compel forgiveness or reconciliation.

Scott's difficulty with processing the five steps became clear as he rode his tricycle around our driveway one Saturday morning.

I stood on the sidewalk at the base of the driveway chatting with our neighbor. Scott angled his handlebars in my direction and maneuvered his trike into my shin.

"Ow!" I looked at my little guy sternly. "That hurt, Scotty."

"I'm sorry, Mommy." He backpedaled the tricycle, and I resumed my adult conversation. Without changing course, he pedaled forward again, crashing into my shin.

"Scott Douglas!" I leaned forward, bringing my stern expression down to his level. "I told you that hurt. Don't drive your tricycle into my leg."

"I'm sorry," he said, looking very much like he wasn't. He began backpedaling again. Without turning his handlebars to the left or the right, he resumed his forward motion, pedaling as fast as his little legs would go. But this time I was ready for impact. I faced him squarely, bent down, and stopped his momentum with a tight grip on the handlebars.

"You are hurting Mommy, and you need to stop right now."

"I'm sorry."

"No. You are not. If you were sorrowful about hurting me, you wouldn't keep doing it." I straightened up and held out my right hand like a traffic cop signaling a stop. "I want to hear the five-step apology right now."

He shrugged his shoulders.

I sighed. Was I expecting too much from a preschooler? I tapped the thumb on my outstretched hand. "The first step is to tell me you're sorry." I stressed the word "first" and wiggled my thumb.

"I'm sorry," he said. This time his eyes suggested he might actually feel remorse.

I tapped my index finger. "I was wrong."

"I. Was. Wrong." Scott sounded repentant.

I tapped my middle finger. "I won't do it again."

"I won't do it again." He parroted the line with convincing conviction.

I smiled with satisfaction at this successful teaching moment and dropped my hand. "Will you forgive me?"

Scott pursed his lips and looked up at the sky. Then he smiled at me. "OK, Mommy. I forgive you."

My neighbor belly laughed as Scott backpedaled, turned his handlebars sharply, and took off down the sidewalk.

My darling little boy made forgiveness a simple task. If only every offender were as easy to forgive. Learning the true meaning of biblical forgiveness helps make things easier when the offence hurts more deeply than a trike to the shin.

Understanding what forgiveness does not require will keep us from wrong thinking and wrong standing. In summary, forgiveness does not require

1. Excusing the offender
2. Confronting the offender
3. Reconciling with the offender
4. Receiving an apology from the offender

Learning what forgiveness does require is equally important. In one of the best presentations I've seen on the subject, UCLA psychiatrist Dr. Stephen Marmer said,

> One of our challenges in understanding this process is that the word *forgiveness* is inadequate to explain a very complex concept. Forgiveness actually embodies three different things, each of which applies to different situations and provides different results. The three types of forgiveness are exoneration, forbearance, and release.[2]

Dr. Marmer defines exoneration as "wiping the slate entirely clean and restoring a relationship to the full state of innocence it had before the harmful actions took place." Making your way through the five-step apology can lead to exoneration. In my experience, relationships with someone you have exonerated grow stronger in the end. For instance, I once met a woman at church, and we immediately connected. We set a coffee date, and she was a no-show. I called her from the coffeehouse and heard road noise when she answered.

"Hi," I said, hoping for the best. "Are you running late?"

"Not really," she said, apparently clueless. "My husband and I are making our way north. I had nothing going on and decided at the last minute to tag along on his business trip."

She had no idea I'd been waiting for her for almost a half hour.

"Did I get the date wrong? I'm here at—"

"Oh no!" She sounded mortified. "I can't believe I totally forgot our coffee date! I. Am. So. Sorry!"

I knew in that moment she was a woman after my own heart. I laughed out loud. "No worries," I said. "The best relationships are forged out of moments like these."

"I was thinking the exact same thing!" she exclaimed, followed by two more sincere apologies. Today, we are the best of friends.

Forbearance doesn't always have the same happy ending as exoneration. Dr. Marmer said, "Forbearance applies when the offender makes a partial apology or mingles their expression of sorrow with blame that you somehow caused them to behave badly." In these cases, he recommends accepting the apology but retaining a degree of watchfulness. "By using forbearance you are able to maintain ties to people who, while far from perfect, are still important to you. Furthermore, in some cases after a sufficient period of good behavior, forbearance can rise to exoneration and full forgiveness."

Of the three types of forgiveness described in Dr. Marmer's presentation, release most closely resembles *aphiēmi*. To lay aside. To let be. To release. The UCLA psychiatrist puts it this way:

> Release does not exonerate the offender. Nor does it require forbearance. It doesn't even demand that you continue the relationship. But it does ask that instead of continuing to define much of your life in terms of the hurt done, you release your bad feelings and your preoccupation with the negative things that have happened to you.

This prominent mental health professional concludes his instruction on release by explaining, it "liberates you from the tyranny of living in the traumatic past even when the other forms of forgiveness (exoneration and forbearance) are not possible."

Sister, let's not just open our clenched fists to release traumatic memories. Let's invert our hands like the young man who showed a missionary his palms-down way to pray. Let's dump the responsibility for judgment and justice onto God's lap. God's commands are always for our good—including his command to forgive.

Unforgiveness Can Become a Bitter Root

The previous chapter focused on the emotional pain of rejection. It troubles your mind, plagues your body, and pierces your spirit. Taking your thoughts captive, renouncing lies, and declaring truth from God's Word is essential for healing. But complete healing will never happen if you allow unforgiveness to germinate. Unforgiveness sets deep roots and grows into a grove of bitterness, which bears rotten fruit like anger, resentment, and fear. Satan greedily grabs the gnarled branches sprouting from bitter roots and uses them as footholds to climb into your heart and rob you of joy and peace.

I've introduced you to every member of my immediate family but one. Between Sarah and Scott, Steve and I welcomed our little fighter, Sam. He came into this world on Leap Day, and the delivery room staff immediately whisked him away. My dear husband followed them in confusion. He remembered that Sarah had been placed in my arms immediately after she was born. Steve returned with the terrifying news that something wasn't right with our baby boy.

"They've called for a neonatologist," he said with obvious concern.

I didn't know what to expect when the specialist arrived, but I never could've prepared myself for the abrasive treatment dished out to me by that man. With no compassion or even a semblance of appropriate bedside manner, the neonatologist told me my baby was going to die. The shock and pain consuming the next several days pushed the encounter far from my mind, but an equally disturbing exchange a few days later dragged that dreadful doctor back into my head and deposited him into my long-term memory.

My obstetrician had performed a cesarean after discovering that Sam presented in the breach position. Due to concern for my physical well-being after major abdominal surgery and the added stress of caring for a special needs infant, he directed the neonatology staff to keep my son for five days after my discharge, which was five days after my surgery.

I visited Sam daily to wrap myself in the gift of every moment I could spend rocking him and singing to him. Four days into the routine of scrubbing and donning a gown to protect the immunocompromised premature babies on the unit, I bumped into the doctor at the entrance. He glared at me.

"Take that baby out of my NICU," he said, using the shortened term for neonatal intensive care unit. "I need more bed space." Then he brushed past me and disappeared down the hall. The impact of his words did not leave with him. They followed me to the coveted crib. I tried to greet my son with my usual, "Hi Sammy. Mommy's here," but my breath caught in my throat, which had knotted up tight. I sat in the familiar rocker and pressed my lips against the top of his head, squeezing my eyes shut. But I couldn't stop the tears.

The nurse handed me a tissue. I nodded my appreciation and fumbled to hold my son securely while dabbing my nose and eyes.

"I'm sorry he said that to you." The nurse placed her hand on my shoulder. "He likes to help preemie babies get stronger and then send them home. I think he just feels helpless because there's nothing he can do for your son."

Sam was born with one too many chromosomes. His brain did not develop well enough to tell his lungs to keep breathing. The nurse was right about one thing: there was nothing the doctor could do. I took Sammy home the next day as planned. He died in my arms near midnight less than two weeks later.

For nearly fifteen years, I had no idea I harbored bitterness in my heart toward that dreadful doctor. Then I took a job in communications and marketing at the children's hospital that ran the satellite NICU in the hospital where I had delivered Sam. My new coworkers invited me to join them for a Starbucks run. Located onsite, the popular coffeehouse was tucked into a hallway marked by a donor plaque. I had previously seen several of these plaques posted around the campus to honor various philanthropists and their contributions. As I stood in line to order my latte, I read the donor's name and felt physical pain in my chest.

Sam's neonatologist and I now worked at the same hospital. The realization paralyzed me. The line moved forward, but I didn't. I stared at the plaque until a coworker called my name and gestured for me to move.

"That doctor was at the satellite NICU when my son was there," I said, pointing to the plaque. "Does he still work here?"

"No, and he didn't leave on the best terms," said one of my coworkers. "In fact, I wouldn't be surprised if that plaque doesn't come down soon."

The relief that washed over me exposed the bitter root of unforgiveness I had buried the day I took Sam home from the hospital. Each time I went for a latte, the pain in my chest cried out for healing. So I started making excuses when my coworkers left for their routine Starbucks run. But then the pain cried out when they left me behind. I knew I had to forgive. I couldn't do it quickly or easily; but eventually, little by little, I was able to release that man and the hurtful things he had said to me. I knew the bitterness had been thoroughly uprooted when I was able to rejoin my coworkers on our coffee break. I readied myself as I entered the hallway with the plaque, believing I wouldn't be affected by the name that no longer had any power over me. The plaque was gone. And so was my pain.

How to Obey the Command to Forgive

God does command us to forgive. But don't worry. Our loving and logical God would never require us to do the impossible. Forgiveness may challenge you to your core, but it's doable. With God, all things are possible—even forgiving the unforgiveable.

When I learned how to sign what became our sisterhood's secret signal, I imagined myself as a stick figure represented by my index finger and God as the hand that swoops in to lift me up. (I did it again just now.) I pictured the same rescue when I reread Psalm 139 again today. "If I dwell by the farthest oceans [as I point to myself and then hold up my right index finger], even there your hand will guide me, and your strength will support me [as I grab my finger with my left hand and pull straight up]."

I'm special. Say it. Sign it. Believe it. God's hand of blessing upon your head confirms it. With his hand on you, forgiveness is not out of reach because nothing lies beyond God's grasp or ability. Not even forgiveness.

When you obey God's command to forgive, you disarm Satan. You break off the gnarled branches that sprouted from bitter roots, and you take away his foothold. You can be free from the negative effects of your offender's sin against you, just as I am free of painful memories from the NICU. I believe God wants to set you free. He wants to help you forgive those who have hurt you—not excuse them but release them, and renounce your right to judge them or seek revenge.

I told you this book would be filled with calls to action. I've challenged you to journal through Psalm 139, and to believe and speak the truth contained in the Manifesto of Acceptance. And now I have another assignment for you. I'd like you to set aside time in a solitary place to pray through the Scripture-based prayer of forgiveness below. Please don't hold on to an offense and allow it to rob you of peace and joy. Send it away—palms down. *Aphiēmi.* Forgiveness is not an emotion. We don't merely feel forgiving. Forgiveness is something we do. It's a decision. We choose to forgive. You may not feel ready to do that today, and that's OK. Mark this page, and ask God for the strength to do it at the right time. I believe he will let you know when you're ready. When the time comes, don't forget about the study documenting the effectiveness of taking Tylenol before recalling a painful rejection. I wish I'd known those research findings before I saw that donor plaque.

Prayer of Forgiveness

To begin this activity, ask God whom you need to forgive and the specific offenses you need to forgive them for. As they come to mind, speak this prayer aloud:

Dear God,

I know you command me to forgive (Col. 3:13b). I understand I must forgive others in order for you to forgive me (Matt. 6:15).

I know you help me obey your commands (Phil. 2:13), and I trust you will help me to forgive. I believe your hand will guide me and your strength will support me. (Ps. 139:10).

Although I can't see your eyes, ears, or mouth, I know you can see, hear, and speak to me. I believe you saw me when this happened to me. I believe you hear me now. Therefore, you know that I don't want to hold on to this offense any longer.

I choose to forgive [*name the offender*] for [*name the specific offense*].

I acknowledge that *his/her* sins and the results of *his/her* actions affected my life and made me feel [*list negative emotions experienced*].

I now release [*name the offender*] and the sins *he/she* committed against me to you, the only righteous judge.

In Jesus's name, I renounce all influences of evil that came through the sins committed against me and through harboring unforgiveness in my heart. Restore me to wholeness and cancel the effects of the sins committed against me. Heal my memories of these past events so that when I think about what happened, I won't experience overwhelming negative feelings toward [*name the offender*].

Thank you, God, for helping me forgive, for healing me from the pain, and for setting me free. Amen.

Chapter Five

I AM
WONDERFULLY MADE

Psalm 139:13–16
13 You made all the delicate, inner parts of my body
and knit me together in my mother's womb.
14 Thank you for making me so wonderfully complex!
Your workmanship is marvelous—how well I know it.
15 You watched me as I was being formed in utter seclusion,
as I was woven together in the dark of the womb.
16 You saw me before I was born.
Every day of my life was recorded in your book.
Every moment was laid out
before a single day had passed.

Two powerful forces are at work to define us: the impressions people draw from our appearance and behaviors, and the core beliefs we hold deep inside about who we really are. Ultimately, our core beliefs have the upper hand at shaping our identity. In the depths of your soul, do you believe what other people say about you, or do you agree with God's view of who you are?

Psalm 139 sheds glorious light on your true identity. If you haven't already done so, please read verses 13–16 aloud. I challenge you to take your declaration a step further by heading to the nearest mirror to speak it with conviction while looking at your delicate, wonderfully complex, marvelous reflection. Before you turn away, give the *I'm Special Sisterhood* secret signal to affirm your God-approved identity. You are beautiful. You belong. You are loved.

The fourth line of the Manifesto of Acceptance addresses who you are inside and out.

I am wonderfully made.

You were knit together by the master craftsman, who watched you and wanted you before you were born. Your existence was anticipated and planned by the Creator of the universe, who laid out every moment of your life before a single day had passed. You are a masterpiece with a unique purpose. Declare the fourth line of the Manifesto aloud.

I am wonderfully made.

Believe it! God made human beings in his image, to be like him. By framing his design for you from the perfect model, God made certain to craft you with precision for a purpose. You are God's masterpiece, equipped with everything needed to do the incredible things God planned for you to do and to be the complex person he created you to be.

I am wonderfully made.

This line of the Manifesto may be the most difficult to believe, but that doesn't make it any less true. Just because someone else seems to have everything you lack doesn't mean you aren't wonderfully made or are any less wonderfully made. We women have a terrible habit of comparing ourselves to other women and coming up short. Comparison robs us of the joy of acceptance. God didn't make you to be like someone else. He made you in his image, to be like him.

I am wonderfully made.

When considering which Bible character to sketch in support of this declaration, I instantly thought of Queen Esther. Very beautiful and lovely, Esther was admired by everyone who saw her. As quickly as I thought of her, however, I began to reconsider. David didn't write Psalm 139:13–16 to extol his rugged good looks. Nor did he write it to commend our Creator for crafting beauty queens. David wrote these four verses to praise God for designing his workmanship for a unique purpose. The lessons in this chapter go way further than skin-deep, so I tried to think of a different Bible character—one who was not *obviously* wonderfully made.

But I kept coming back to Esther.

I realized God made her beautiful because she *had* to be beautiful. In other words, Esther's purpose was connected to her beauty. If she hadn't caught the king's eye, she wouldn't have been in a position to save her people. I also realized that no one is immune to rejection. For all the times I'm tempted to think my longing to belong would be satisfied if only I had a flawless face and fabulous figure, Esther's story proves otherwise. Loneliness hides extremely well beneath a lovely veneer.

Let's look at how Queen Esther confronted the destructive power of isolation and boldly exposed her true self, regardless of the consequences.

A Secret Identity

The Old Testament book of Esther chronicles a young woman's rise from orphaned exile to Persian queen. While Esther's story may sound like a rags-to-riches fairy tale, she had little in common with Cinderella—other than a secret identity.

Snatched from her cousin's home in the citadel of Susa, Esther was one of many virgins taken from their families into the king's harem for his pleasure. Yes, King Xerxes did set the royal crown on Esther's head and declare her queen, but she didn't live happily ever after as his one true love. Esther became one of numerous wives and concubines belonging to the king.

Can you imagine what life must have been like for Esther? I don't think it's a stretch to suggest she experienced loneliness and insecurity. As a child, Esther grieved the death of both parents. As a young woman, she lost the familiar surroundings of her home. As a bride, she had no choice but to share her husband's bed with numerous women.

Loneliness and insecurity feed on instability and uncertainty.

To make Esther's sense of isolation worse, she couldn't tell her husband about her family background. Her cousin Mordecai, who raised her after her mother and father died, insisted that Esther should hide her Jewish roots. Intimacy suffers when we can't be honest and vulnerable.

Loneliness and insecurity crave genuine intimacy.

Esther's inability to connect with her husband didn't emanate from hollow lies she believed about their relationship. Her isolation was legitimate. By law, Esther had no right whatsoever to approach her husband. If the king didn't call for her, she couldn't see him. If she tried to see him uninvited, he could have her executed. I can't even imagine living with the knowledge that my husband could command my death if I came to him without his permission.

Mordecai must have known the law, but the possibility of his cousin's execution didn't keep him from asking Esther to spontaneously approach the king. He was desperate.

One of the king's officials, Haman, despised Mordecai and had finagled an edict out of the king to put all Jews to death. King Xerxes had no idea he had given the order for his wife, her family, and her entire race to be annihilated. Neither did Haman.

Upon hearing news of the king's decree, Mordecai decided that the time was right for Esther to reveal her roots. He sent word directing her to appear before the king uninvited and beg for mercy on behalf of the Jewish people—*her* people.

Esther sent one of her attendants to Mordecai with her response:

All the king's officials and even the people in the prov-
inces know that anyone who appears before the king in
his inner court without being invited is doomed to die
unless the king holds out his gold scepter. And the king
has not called for me to come to him for thirty days.

Thirty days.

Esther had zero contact with her husband for thirty days. Had
he been with other women? Did he think of her at all? Would he
hold out his gold scepter . . . or would he call for her death?

Mordecai replied to Esther with these words:

Don't think for a moment that because you're in the
palace you will escape when all other Jews are killed. If
you keep quiet at a time like this, deliverance and relief
for the Jews will arise from some other place, but you
and your relatives will die. Who knows if perhaps you
were made queen for just such a time as this?

Who knows?

Esther was wonderfully made for a specific purpose. Her
flawless face and fabulous figure arrested the king's attention,
but God envisioned more than eye candy when he knit Esther
together in her mother's womb. In her role as queen, Esther offered
her people the only open door through which to plead for their
lives. But would walking through that door cost Esther her own
life? Mustering courage to approach King Xerxes wasn't simply a
matter of refusing to feel unwanted or neglected. If her husband
rejected her, she would die.

Each time Esther put on her royal robes and set a crown upon
her head, she dressed in reminders of her desirability. Would her
appearance alone convince the king to hold out his gold scepter?

Fear and doubt must have coursed through Esther's mind. Was she really made queen for such a time as this? Who knew?

Thirty days is a long time.

Esther sent Mordecai this response: "Go and gather together all the Jews of Susa and fast for me. Do not eat or drink for three days, night or day. My maids and I will do the same. And then, though it is against the law, I will go in to see the king. If I must die, I must die."

Whenever I see the word "fast," I also think "pray." Oddly, the word "pray" doesn't appear anywhere in the book of Esther. What's more, the book never mentions God nor contains a single "Thus saith the Lord" proclamation. However, God's hand is clearly at work—from the strange coincidences surrounding King Xerxes's sleepless night, which led to him honoring Mordecai the very day Haman had plotted to have him executed, to the timing of Xerxes's return from the palace garden to find Haman falling all over Esther, pleading for his life, which the king abruptly ended by hanging Haman on the very gallows Haman had set up for Mordecai.

While Esther's call to a unified fast didn't reference prayer, she clearly intended to move the hand of God. The strange coincidences I mentioned above occurred during Esther's fast. Over the course of three days with no food or drink, God answered Esther in ways she never could have imagined. Not only did the king hold out the gold scepter, but he also accepted two consecutive dinner invitations and repeatedly offered to grant Esther's requests—even up to half his kingdom. Please don't miss the significance of Xerxes's offer to his queen. He offered Esther half his kingdom.

Half his. Half hers.

Equally his and equally no one else's but hers.

Xerxes elevated Esther to such a high position of worth that no one could match her status. No other woman could come close to what she alone shared with her husband.

If loneliness and insecurity make you feel unwanted or useless, you might want to fast and pray. I'm not suggesting you go three days without food or drink—especially if you've never fasted before. Maybe start by skipping the TV show you look forward to watching every week and spending that time in prayer instead. Draw close to the one who created you with precision and purpose. He will satisfy your hunger to be valued and quench your thirst for intimacy. You could also pull out your journal during your fast. Working your way through our next set of verses from Psalm 139 may help reveal the purpose for which God created you. Psalm 139:13–16 provides the framework for an important declaration about your significance. This declaration is every bit as true for you as it was for Esther. Why not say it out loud now?

I am wonderfully made.

Fourth Journal Prompt: Psalm 139:13–16

I have been asking much of you. I asked you to learn American Sign Language for "I'm special" and rehearse it as a reminder of your great worth. I asked you to learn a seven-line Manifesto and silence dead-end thoughts by declaring its life-giving truth. I asked you to read Psalm 139 aloud and commit to journaling through its verses. As if that wasn't enough, I asked you to take the difficult step of forgiving those who have offended you. Even if you have undertaken these activities with little confidence or avoided them altogether, I believe God has placed this book in your hands for such a time as this. You aren't reading this page by accident. God recorded every day of your life and laid out every moment before a single day had passed—including this moment right now.

Before asking anything of you, I asked God to lead you to discover the joy of acceptance. I asked God to reveal supernatural keys to unlock the truth of your extreme value and esteemed identity. I asked God to empower you to claim your rightful place of belonging as his beloved child. I'm grinning with assurance that my prayers are being answered. I believe God is equipping you to walk in victory even now. This is your time to reprogram negative thought patterns and make a habit of right thinking and right standing.

Perhaps more than any of our journaling activities so far, working through our next set of verses will center your mind on how amazing you are and how much potential for greatness lives inside of you. As you meditate on Psalm 139:13–16, make a home in your head for truth. Evict any lies living there by declaring, "I am wonderfully made." Believe and speak what God says about your inherent value. There's no better cure for flare-ups of chronic rejection issues. If you've based your identity on impressions drawn from your appearance and behaviors, it's time to agree with God's view of who you are. Queen Esther knew she was wonderfully made, not simply because everyone admired her beauty, but because God had created her for a unique purpose—a purpose she risked her life to fulfill.

It's time again to set this book aside for a journaling activity. As you meet with God, ask him to reveal the purpose for which he created you. Listen closely and record what you hear him saying. God made you for such a time as this. Don't wait another minute to ask what comes next.

Who I AM Is and Who I Am

In Exodus 3, God called Moses to lead Israel out of Egypt. Moses looked inward and came up short. Born a Jew, raised an Egyptian prince, and living in self-imposed exile, he had little confidence in his qualifications as a leader. So he protested to God, "Who am I to appear before Pharaoh? Who am I to lead the people of Israel out of Egypt?"

In response, God didn't motivate Moses to tap into his inner strength or inspire him to acknowledge hidden greatness. Instead, God redirected Moses's focus, saying, "I will be with you" and "I am the one."

So then, Moses protested to the tune of "Who are you?" His objection to accepting God's assignment begged the question of identity—both his and God's.

God replied with a simple declaration: "*I AM WHO I AM.*" One commentary explains that *I AM*

> signifies the real being of God, his self-existence, and that he is the Being of beings; as also it denotes his eternity and immutability, and his constancy and faithfulness in fulfilling his promises, for it includes all time, past, present, and to come; and the sense is, not only I am what I am at present, but I am what I have been, and I am what I shall be, and shall be what I am.[1]

Moses argued his inadequacy and lamented his limitations. God promised his presence and proclaimed the infinite nature of his being. When you and I feel less than equipped for our calling, God responds to our self-doubt with assurances of his all-sufficiency. We can say with confidence, "I am wonderfully made. God equipped me with everything I need to be the person he created me to be. Who *I AM* is makes who I am marvelous."

As demonstrated by the four lines we've learned so far in our Manifesto of Acceptance, Psalm 139 supports the gravity of God's identity. Developed from themes drawn directly from Psalm 139:1–16, the first two lines of the Manifesto focus on God, and the next two focus on who we are because of him.

God knows me.

He is always with me.

I am not invisible.

I am wonderfully made.

Through the structure of Psalm 139, God seems to say, "Look at me, and then look at how I look at you." This perspective drastically changes our view of who we are, especially if we look long and hard at God.

In the appendix, you'll find the worksheet "Who *I AM* Is and Who I Am." I designed it as a tool to magnify knowledge of God and expand comprehension of your true identity. The assignment calls on you to write out Bible verses that contradict what you currently believe about yourself and God, and then write a brief statement acknowledging the contradictions and explaining why you no longer believe the lies. (For a resource with verses describing God's character and thoughts about you, visit ShawnaMarieBryant.com/WhoIAm.) I challenge you to reprogram your brain by memorizing the verses you write on the worksheet. No more defaulting to what other people say about you, sis. It's your time to believe God's opinion of who you are.

Why I Am Who I Am

My mother gave me an awesome hammer when I moved away from home. At a glance, it seemed like a tool with one purpose, but unscrewing the handle from the hammerhead turned it into a screwdriver. Twisting off the end of the screwdriver revealed a Phillip's screwdriver hidden in its shaft. People can be like that multipurpose tool. I know of talented entertainers who can sing, dance, and act. I know of professional football players who left the gridiron for the ballpark to play a second sport professionally. I know of prominent women with all the favored qualities: beauty, intelligence, poise, and strength—women like Queen Esther.

God has his reasons for fashioning a woman like Esther. He also has his reasons for fashioning a woman like you. God made you the way he made you for *his* purposes. He has a plan for your life, and he created you to fit perfectly into *his* plan. When you pursue a plan of your own, you risk the futility of trying to become something God never created you to be. Even if you will never be a queen—at least when it comes to being married to a king—that doesn't mean you aren't special. You are royally special. If you're like me, you sometimes need a reminder of your inheritance as a child of the King.

I met up with a few girlfriends at an Italian deli on a day when I desperately needed to acknowledge who I was created to be. The lunch hour crowd buzzed with an energy I hardly noticed, and my girlfriends engaged in animated conversation while I fiddled with my food. When their voices lulled, I expressed frustration with my pursuit of God's plan for my life.

"I feel like a pawn on God's chessboard." I was tired of yielding my desires to God's will, tired of running into roadblocks to realizing my dreams, and tired of obeying God without receiving recognition or reward. "It's like I'm sitting there in my little square, and God picks me up and plunks me down wherever he wants."

"You're not a pawn, Shawna," said one of my friends as she shook her head. "Pawns are expendable. You're the queen."

I can't help but smile at the memory. She was right. I'm the queen! You're the queen too—even if you're nothing like Esther. You are wonderfully made to be who you are. Look long and hard at God, and then look at how he looks at you. Try not to look around. Comparing yourself to someone created for a different purpose can leave you discontented—even disgruntled—with God.

Both my college roommates stood nearly six feet tall, with long legs to die for. They towered over me by seven inches. Friends poked lighthearted fun at my height. It wasn't the first time I felt less than adequate in stature. That teasing bumped up against a tender spot and bruised me. I gave the playful jests of my college friends too much space in my head. One particular comment consumed me: "When it came to handing out legs, God shorted you."

I decided to blame God for my lacking stature. After all, I'm not responsible for my height. He is the reason I'm not tall with legs to die for. Playing the blame game set me up like a dodge ball target against perfectly aimed truth. I couldn't dash away from Paul's pointed question in Romans 9:20: "Who are you, a mere human being, to argue with God? Should the thing that was created say to the one who created it, 'Why have you made me like this?'"

Neither could I dodge the obvious answer to Isaiah 45:9: "Does a clay pot argue with its maker? Does the clay dispute with the one who shapes it, saying, 'Stop, you're doing it wrong!' Does the pot exclaim, 'How clumsy can you be?'"

God has a right and a reason to make me short and my roommates tall. He has a right and a reason to make Esther beautiful and Rahab bold. He has a right and a reason to make a clay pot like me and another one like you. He shaped us to receive his Spirit, which he generously poured out through Jesus Christ.

Paul described God's indwelling presence with another pottery metaphor: "But this beautiful treasure is contained in us—cracked pots made of earth and clay—so that the transcendent character of this power will be clearly seen as coming from God and not from us" (2 Cor. 4:7 VOICE).

We tend to criticize the visible imperfections of the clay pot more readily than we praise the transcendent character hidden within. Seeing ourselves through the eyes of Creator God redirects our focus from external appearances and behaviors to the beautiful treasure inside us. Looking long and hard at God, and then looking at how he looks at us, reinforces our identity as royal heirs in God's kingdom.

When I was in my tender teens, my youth director lead our group of junior high and high schoolers through an exercise that supported having a healthy self-image. After handing each student a 3 × 5 card and a pen, the youth director asked us to list three things we didn't like about ourselves. I only remember one of them. My legs. Then the director told a tale that went something like this.

Tale of the Warm Fuzzies

Once upon a time in a kingdom full of love and kindness, people everywhere expressed appreciation for one another every day. Young and old throughout the kingdom shared joy and laughter by continually giving and receiving warm fuzzies. The gift of warm fuzzies made them feel special in every way.

One day, a wicked sorceress snuck into the kingdom with an evil plan.

"Why do you keep giving away your warm fuzzies?" she asked the first person she saw. "Aren't you afraid you're going to run out? Why don't you keep the warm fuzzies to yourself and give cold pricklies instead?"

The wicked sorceress handed the unsuspecting man a cold prickly and then vanished, leaving him all alone. He did not like the way the cold prickly made him feel, so he gave it to the first person he saw. The woman who received it had planned to give him a warm fuzzy, but once she felt the sting of the cold prickly, she gave it right back to him.

The wicked sorceress went about giving cold pricklies to everyone she saw, and they too felt the sting. The people of the kingdom withdrew from one another so they could avoid receiving yet another cold prickly. They soon forgot about the warm fuzzies. Stung by bitterness and fear, the kingdom was no longer full of love and kindness.

One day a prince arrived. The first person to see him gave him a cold prickly, but the prince refused to take it. She gave it to him again, but still the prince would not receive it. Instead, he gave her a warm fuzzy.

"Why did you give me a warm fuzzy?" she asked. "Aren't you afraid you'll run out?"

"The more I give away, the more I have to give," said the prince. "I will never run out of warm fuzzies because I am a child of the King."

The prince gave the woman another warm fuzzy. And another. And another. She felt like she did not deserve them, but they filled her heart with the joy of acceptance.

"Don't be discouraged, and don't be afraid," said the prince. "You will never run out of warm fuzzies because you are a child of the King."

Overflowing with gifts from the prince, the woman gave a warm fuzzy to the first person she saw. She could not contain the gifts, so she went about giving warm fuzzies to everyone she could find. She did not run out of warm fuzzies, and her heart began to overflow with love and kindness.

The sorceress grew angry and cornered the woman. "Who do you think you are?" she hissed. "Why do you think you are special? This is what you deserve!" The sorceress gave her a cold prickly, but she refused to take it.

"I do not receive your cold prickly, and I do not believe your lies," the woman said to the sorceress. "I learned from the prince that I will never run out of warm fuzzies because I am a child of the King."

With that, the sorceress withdrew for an opportune time.

After telling this allegory, my youth director instructed us to label the 3 × 5 card "Cold Pricklies" and tape it to the nape of our necks. If I had known my list would be broadcast to my entire youth group, I never would've mentioned my short legs. I hated wearing that label, and suddenly I was responsible for attaching it to myself. Next, we each received a sheet of paper labeled "Warm Fuzzies," and another student taped it just below the card.

We spent the rest of the evening mingling, reading each other's core beliefs about our identity, and writing words of encouragement on each other's backs. I tucked the paper I received that night into my wallet. Then, a few years later in college, God reminded me of my tattered warm fuzzy. Though inundated with covetous complaints about my tall roommates, God gently embraced me like a loving father drawing his little girl onto his knee. At his prompting, I pulled the warm fuzzy from my wallet, unfolded it, and smoothed the creases. I heard the voice of my Creator as I read my favorite entry. "You have great legs."

Much more than the encouraging words on the tattered sheet from my youth group, I treasure warm fuzzies from God. Far beyond complimenting outward appearances and behaviors, God's words of affirmation settle forever our favored status as children of the King.

Discovering the joy of acceptance rests on two pillars of truth:

1. I always have and always will be who God says I am.
2. I always have and always will belong to God.

God understands our longing to belong. As early as the Genesis account of Adam and Eve, the Creator acknowledged man's need for a suitable helper to keep him from being alone. Even so, no human being can guarantee to never leave us, and no human being has the power to define us. Only God can and does.

In Chapter Three, I called out abandonment as one of the biggest bandits responsible for robbing us of the joy of acceptance. Its primary accomplice is the identity thief. God confronts these coconspirators in the opening verses of Psalm 139. That's why the first two lines in the Manifesto of Acceptance address identity (God knows me) and abandonment (He is always with me). I intentionally aligned those verses with sketches of Bible characters who wrestled with issues of identity (the woman at the well) and abandonment (Joshua). The next two lines of the Manifesto also arrest these twin bandits. Declaring "I am not invisible" and "I am wonderfully made" with confidence plants seeds of truth about who you are and how valuable you are. Nurturing these seeds cultivates healthy core beliefs that bring a harvest of right thinking and right standing.

Rahab wore the shameful label of prostitute, but God always knew her as a brave hero. He exalted her as the honorable mother of Boaz. Although Esther wore a crown, she had been separated from family and ignored by her husband for weeks on end, but God never abandoned her. He established her with royal influence at just the right time.

What labels do you wear? Are they warm fuzzy words or cold prickly jabs? Just like the prince in the Tale of the Warm Fuzzies, you can refuse to accept the hurtful labels. Just like the woman who rebuked the sorceress, you can claim your rightful place of belonging as a child of the King.

I designed the "Who *I AM* Is and Who I Am" worksheet in the appendix to bless you with warm fuzzies. Your completed worksheet may become like my tattered treasure from youth group. Read it for descriptions of God's marvelous works, and believe you are beautiful. Read it for documentation of God's covenant of faithfulness, and believe you belong. Read it for expressions of God's ultimate sacrifice, and believe you are loved.

Wearing a Label versus Expressing Identity

New York Times best-selling author Priscilla Shirer, a favorite Bible teacher of mine, received torrents of criticism for comments she made in a video posted to Facebook. The controversy erupted from sparks of misunderstanding about identifying—or rather *not* identifying—in a certain manner. The segment, which garnered more than ten million views on Facebook in fewer than five months, shows Priscilla speaking from a large platform in front of a live audience.

> I do not describe myself as a black woman because that gives too much power to my blackness. I don't want my race to be the describing adjective of who I am as a woman. I am not a black woman. I am a Christian woman who happens to be black. . . . It's the job of your adjective to describe the noun of who you are. If there's gonna be an adjective describing me, it's not gonna be my race; it's going to be I'm a woman who believes in every single thing that my God has declared to be true, and I will stand firmly on the promises of his Word because I will be girded in truth.[2]

The fact that this statement offended thousands supports my opinion that today's culture gives too much power to labels. People can attach more than a dozen descriptive, accurate labels to me, but that doesn't mean I have to identify by a single one of them—even if the label represents a big part of who I am.

Awash in the backlash after the video clip went viral, Priscilla clarified her intent via Twitter to her large social media following:

> I'm unbelievably proud to be a black woman. My identification with the African American community—the struggles and the triumphs—is something that I value

greatly. Within the context of the entire message I was giving at the time, my only intention was to make the point that no aspect of life should ever define a believer MORE than their relationship w/Christ. I should have been more clear.[3]

Pricilla's intent reminds me of the apostle Paul, who refused to identify by his race and went much further in discounting its value than Priscilla did. He undoubtedly offended people with these choice words:

> I am a pure-blooded citizen of Israel and a member of the tribe of Benjamin—a real Hebrew if there ever was one! . . .
>
> I once thought these things were valuable, but now I consider them worthless because of what Christ has done. Yes, everything else is worthless when compared with the infinite value of knowing Christ Jesus my Lord. For his sake I have discarded everything else, counting it all as garbage, so that I could gain Christ. (Phil. 3:5, 7–8)

Paul died to every label but one: Christ lives in me. Pricilla chose to identify by one label more than any other: Christian. Exalting your identity in Christ over every other label reinforces God's opinion of who you are. God sees you like no one else can— not even you see yourself as clearly as your Creator does. He sees what you are becoming—not what you are. No matter how you appear or what you accomplish, God's view of you will never change. He made you for a purpose for just such a time as this. Sister, you are wonderfully made.

GOD'S COUNTLESS
THOUGHTS ARE FOR ME

Psalm 139:17–18
17 How precious are your thoughts about me, O God.
They cannot be numbered!
18 I can't even count them;
they outnumber the grains of sand!
And when I wake up,
you are still with me!

Thus far, we have been progressing through Psalm 139 by study-ing four verses at a time. The sixteen verses covered in the four previous chapters have taken us more than halfway through the Manifesto of Acceptance. We have now arrived at the fifth line.

God's countless thoughts are for me.

This chapter goes a shorter distance through Psalm 139, with just two verses. Please pause to read them aloud now. As you declare Psalm 139:17–18, taste the sweetness of the tender word used to describe God's thoughts about you. Swallow the satisfac-tion of knowing his precious thoughts endear you to him. God loves you to the moon and back. He thinks you are beyond special. I can't help but picture the *I'm Special Sisterhood* secret signal and see your Heavenly Father lifting you up with his thoughts about you. I invite you to picture it too as you declare the newly introduced line of our Manifesto.

God's countless thoughts are for me.

God's thoughts of you bring him such joy that he rejoices over you with gladness and exults over you with singing. I can guess some of his lyrics based on what he says about you in Psalm 139. The Creator of the universe is crazy about you!

God's countless thoughts are for me.

Imagine scooping a handful of sand and dropping it one grain at a time. Each grain represents one of God's thoughts. Imagine counting the grains of sand like sheep to fall asleep. You drift into slumber and awaken hours later with your hand still full of sand. You haven't begun to number God's precious thoughts.

God's countless thoughts are for me.

This promise makes me wish my thoughts about myself were better aligned with God's thoughts about me. Bill Johnson, pastor of Bethel Church in Redding, California, says, "I can't afford to have thoughts in my head about me that God doesn't have in his." Why invest in toxic thoughts? I'm reminded of the slogan: a mind is a terrible thing to waste.[1] Renouncing the lies resounding in our heads and canceling their negative effects takes energy. Considering the losses wrong thinking inflicts on our self-worth, the energy is well spent.

Think about what you think about yourself. If your thoughts are less than precious, they don't align with God's. So take them captive! Instead, think about what God thinks about you. He not only has lots and lots of thoughts *about* you; his thoughts are also *for* you. He is in your corner—even when you don't see it that way.

Joseph, the Bible character known for his multicolored dream coat, learned the hard way that God's thoughts are always intended for our good.

Intended for Good

I'm accustomed to hearing patient people be compared to Job. The Bible character known for his undue hardship certainly endured severe losses and pain, but from what I can tell by reading the text, Job's suffering most likely took place over less than a year. It may even have resolved after a few short months. The patience of Joseph, however, carried him through years of slavery in a foreign country. Years of incarceration for a crime he didn't commit. Years of living far from his father and his home.

Joseph's brothers sold him into slavery as a teenager, and he didn't break free from those bonds until he became governor of Egypt at the age of thirty. Joseph wasn't reunited with his father until at least nine more years had passed. But through it all, he had the "patience of Job." Joseph never cursed God and always lived above reproach.

Joseph's status shifted from favorite son to foreign slave soon after telling his brothers about dreams they didn't want to hear.

> "Listen to this dream," he said. "We were out in the field, tying up bundles of grain. Suddenly my bundle stood up, and your bundles all gathered around and bowed low before mine!"
>
> His brothers responded, "So you think you will be our king, do you? Do you actually think you will reign over us?" And they hated him all the more because of his dreams and the way he talked about them. (Gen. 37:6–8)

A short time later, Joseph had a similar dream in which the sun, moon, and eleven stars (the number of his brothers) bowed down to him. This time, Joseph told his father as well as his brothers. His father responded with reproach.

"Will your mother and I and your brothers actually
come and bow to the ground before you?" But while his
brothers were jealous of Joseph, his father wondered
what the dreams meant. (Gen. 37:10–11)

I imagine Joseph must have wondered what it all meant, too—
especially when his brothers ripped off the beautiful robe his
father had given him and sold him to traders who took him to
Egypt, about 250 miles away. As the caravan of camels and mer-
chants led Joseph further and further from home, his thoughts
must have wrestled with confusion. His dreams had been real
enough to rile his brothers and bewilder his father, but the reality
of his present nightmare made his dreams hard to believe. Joseph
had grown up hearing about the promises God had made to his
father, Jacob; his grandfather, Isaac; and his great-grandfather,
Abraham. For the most part, these patriarchs modeled trusting
God through deeply challenging circumstances. Their example
served Joseph well when his dreams were shattered.

Upon arrival in Egypt, Joseph was purchased by Potiphar,
captain of the guard for Pharaoh, the king of Egypt. Joseph served
Potiphar like a butler, with administrative responsibility over the
captain's household and property. Potiphar's wife noticed the
handsome young man taking care of her husband's affairs and
lustfully came on to Joseph—relentlessly.

Joseph refused her, saying, "How could I do such a wicked
thing? It would be a great sin against God" (Gen. 39:9).

Though unjustly sold by his brothers, Joseph treated his slave
owner with respect. Though pressured day after day to sleep with
a powerful woman, Joseph refused her advances. Though living
apart from his community of faith, Joseph chose to continually
honor God.

Joseph's nightmare intensified when Potiphar's wife cornered him alone. Grabbing him by the cloak, she demanded that he sleep with her. He tore himself from her unwanted embrace and left his cloak in her clutches as he dashed out the door. Potiphar's wife held the only evidence she needed to condemn an innocent man of attempted rape. First, she called out to her servants and conveyed her concocted story. Next, she kept the cloak to prove her fabricated fib to her husband when he came home.

"That Hebrew slave you've brought into our house tried to come in and fool around with me," she said. "But when I screamed, he ran outside, leaving his cloak with me!" (Gen. 39:17–18).

Furious at Joseph's alleged assault on his wife, the captain of Pharaoh's guard threw Joseph into prison with no corroborating evidence or trial. What happened to Joseph's dreams? No one bows to an imprisoned slave accused of attempting to rape his master's wife.

You and I have the benefit of looking back at Joseph's unfolding story from beginning to end. We can see how one thing led to another to land him as governor over all of Egypt. Since we can read Genesis 37–50 in one sitting, we can trace God's hand through it all and see that he was up to something good. In the midst of it, however, Joseph had to trust God to work things out for good.

Just as Potiphar had recognized and employed Joseph's administrative expertise, the prison warden also noticed Joseph's proficiency with managing people and affairs. He gave Joseph charge over all the other prisoners as well as the prison's day-to-day operations. Joseph's status shifted again. The favorite son turned foreign slave transitioned from falsely accused to favored administrator.

Joseph somehow sensed the Lord's loving presence through all his trials. From the hateful actions of his jealous brothers to the immorality of his slave owner's wife, Joseph unduly suffered the consequences of others' bad behavior. And yet he never blamed or rejected God. His resilience astounds me. His faithfulness inspires me. His patient endurance encourages me. I'm reminded of one of my go-to memory verses when my patience is stretched thin:

> For everything that was written in the past was written to teach us, so that through the endurance taught in the Scriptures and the encouragement they provide we might have hope. (Rom. 15:4 NIV)

An Old Testament Bible character like Joseph didn't have the benefit of a New Testament memory verse like my go-to from Paul's letter to the Romans. I'm grateful Joseph's story was written to teach us that God is at work in the most unlikely circumstances.

Genesis 40 provides yet another example of Joseph's unshakeable faith while in the throes of disappointment. While unjustly imprisoned, he accurately interpreted the dreams of two fellow prisoners. One interpretation revealed the prisoner would be released in three days and restored to his position in service to the king of Egypt. Joseph asked the man to mention him to Pharaoh in hopes that he, too, would gain freedom. But the man forgot about Joseph—for two full years. Month after month for twenty-four months, Joseph remained in prison, and yet he never stopped trusting God's promise to raise him up to a position of authority and honor. More than a dozen years after Joseph revealed his dreams to his father and brothers, he continued to believe their implausible interpretation.

The freed prisoner finally remembered Joseph when Pharaoh expressed an urgent need for someone to interpret a couple of his distressing dreams. Joseph's accurate interpretations of Pharaoh's dreams led to his installment as governor. In that position, he administrated the gathering and storing of grain for the severe famine God prepared and Joseph predicted.

Finally, Joseph's own dreams had the chance to come true.

Sent by their father to Egypt to buy food, Joseph's eleven brothers bowed low before the governor, with no idea they looked a lot like bundles of grain. But Joseph didn't remind them of his dreams when he revealed his identity. Neither did he lord his authority over them—even though they cowered before him, speechless. Instead, Joseph told his brothers not to be angry with themselves for selling him into slavery. He encouraged them with his conviction that God had sent him ahead of them to save many lives during the famine. Joseph assured his brothers that God was responsible for his exile in Egypt, not them.

If you are feeling forgotten by God, if your circumstances seem to contradict his promises, if your dreams have been shattered through no fault of your own, be encouraged by Joseph's resilience and trust. Learn from his example of patient endurance and unwavering faith. Believe God can redeem the harmful actions of others to set you up for success. Speak the truth in the fifth line of the Manifesto of Acceptance.

God's countless thoughts are for me.

Fifth Journal Prompt: Psalm 139:17–18

In this book's opening pages, I laid out my plan to help you climb from the pit of an unmet longing. I issued a warning that you would continually collide with a call to believe and speak. I hope you've grown more comfortable with making declarations, because I have another word of caution for you now. Accepting my call to action might make you look illogical and feel foolish—especially when you declare impossibilities as certainties. Wrap your mind around one of my favorite promises from the Bible:

> No eye has seen, no ear has heard, and no mind has imagined what God has prepared for those who love him. (1 Cor. 2:9)

Will you dare to believe and speak what no mind can conceive?

Since childhood, I have openly shared what I believe about Jesus Christ. Even though my outspoken faith has invited ridicule at times, I shamelessly talk about the gospel. However, I haven't always been willing to tell others about God's promises to me. Life got pretty rough for Joseph after he let his brothers know they would all bow down to him one day. I perceived his plight as a sign to keep a lid on my God-given dreams. Besides, declaring promises as though they've already transpired forces me to stand against the reality of my current situation—or it sends me into a trust fall.

Now that I'm further on my faith walk, I no longer fear the repercussions of declaring revelations of truth. I've made myself look downright silly sharing what I've heard from God. These days, I believe and speak with confidence that God will do what he says he will do. My verbalized convictions give him the opportunity to show off. I'll admit I still struggle to believe and speak God's promises when he gives me an impossible dream. Proclaiming the great things God has in store for me invites the smack down of others' disbelief. Thankfully, when hit by jabs like "Who does she think she is?" I can pull myself up because I *know* who I am— beloved daughter of the Most High God!

God's countless thoughts are for me.

It's time to take the five familiar steps through Psalm 139. As you prepare to journal what you learn from verses 17–18, ask God to reveal at least one or two of the countless, precious thoughts he has for you. Please set aside this book temporarily to spend time thinking about what God is thinking about you.

God's Thoughts Matter Most

God's countless thoughts are for me. This line in the Manifesto has helped me control my rejection reflex. Believing God thinks precious thoughts about me stilled my knee-jerk tendency to recoil with rejection upon the slightest provocation. I've learned to make a conscious choice to presume rather than assume.

An assumption almost always involves judgment. It reaches a conclusion without a full grasp of the facts, forming belief without proof. A presumption, on the other hand, establishes belief based on likely outcomes. For example, a presumption of innocence implies a person is not guilty unless and until solid evidence supports guilt beyond a reasonable doubt. Presumptions shift the burden of proof from assuming the worst to assuming the best.

Why do we fall into the habit of assuming the worst?

My daughter, Sarah, didn't have a behavior problem in elementary school. She had a sit-down-be-quiet-and-stay-focused problem. Her third-grade teacher had little patience for Sarah's hyperactivity and sent her to the principal's office on a regular basis. I spent a great deal of time on her elementary school campus, helping out in the classroom and attending sporting events. One Friday afternoon, I ran into the principal. Sarah had made multiple trips to his office by then. He made an off-the-cuff comment I remember clearly, and I can still picture the corridor we were standing in when he said, "With some children, you can't be an armchair parent."

I had no idea what that meant, but it sounded like a reprimand. The principal seemed to think that I sat around with my feet up rather than actively parenting my child. I knew how hard I worked to discipline Sarah, but the principal's careless comment challenged my belief. The armchair accusation leveled lies at me, and the enemy pounced at the opportunity to knock me down with negative self-talk. *He's right to think that about you. You're a bad mom. You failed at parenting.* The enemy leveraged my vulnerabilities as a mom raising a high-maintenance child. Blindsided by an ignorant assumption, I struggled to focus on the truth. *He*

has no evidence to support that allegation. I'm not guilty as charged.
I'm doing my best.

Several months later, I was reclining in front of the television while the kids were playing in their rooms. I heard a clap of thunder and noticed my son had left his gardening toys outside.

"Scotty," I hollered. "Please bring your toys inside. It's about to rain."

"OK, Momma," he called back, and hurried out the sliding glass door. I returned to watching my TV program.

Within minutes, the heavens let loose a torrent of rain. I hopped up and noticed the yard was empty. I called Scott's name out into the rainstorm, but he didn't answer. I hurried to the garage, where I found my preschooler sitting on the concrete floor, taking off his wet shoes. His child-size wheelbarrow, rake, and shovel were lined up to drip dry against the garage wall behind him. My eyes widened in disbelief. My son was barely three years old. He had done everything perfectly without any supervision. I walked inside and plopped on the couch, incredulous. I had only known how to parent Sarah. I had never experienced this ease. As I propped my feet back up, I said aloud, "So that's what armchair parenting is."

Sometimes people, like my daughter's principal, assume the worst about us. They draw conclusions without facts. However, sometimes we assume the worst about ourselves—even to the point of imagining negative thoughts in the minds of other people. My girlfriend calls it M.S.U.ing, short for Making. Stuff. Up. She angles her head, shakes her finger, and says, "Shawna, you're M.S.U.ing again. Stop making stuff up."

I'm a regular at the gym, and I've reached the point of dreading January. The gym crawls with rookies fulfilling their New Year's resolutions. I adjust my workout to avoid competing with other bodies for my favorite cardio machines and weight-lifting equipment. The crowd thins to its normal size by month's end, and I'm free to resume my regular routine.

Shortly after the holiday season ended a few years ago, the flu knocked me down for a good two weeks. Even after I recovered, I didn't have the strength for my early morning workout. I remember lamenting to a friend, "Those people at my gym are probably thinking I'm one of those newbies who joins with good intentions and then fails to keep her New Year's resolution."

She shook her head and said with matter-of-fact indifference, "Those people aren't thinking about you at all."

I can't help but laugh at the memory. My auto-response back then was to deflate at the thought of not being missed. Now I grin at the absurdity of M.S.U.ing. The thoughts other people have about me—assuming those thoughts even exist—may or may not be precious, but they simply don't matter as much as God's thoughts. God's thoughts matter most. Caring too much about the thoughts of others can be harmful, even when they assume the very best about me.

Bill Johnson says, "If you don't live by the praise of men, you won't die by their criticism."

In her book *Uninvited*, Lysa Terkuerst writes, "At the core of who we are we crave the acceptance that comes from being loved. To satisfy this longing we will either be a grasper of God's love or a grabber of people's love. If we grasp the full love of Christ, we won't grab at other things to fill us."[2]

I pray to have the heart of Joseph. Even when his master chucked the presumption of innocence and threw him into jail, Joseph didn't let wrong assumptions deter him from trusting God. Even when his brothers' thoughts toward him were meant for evil, Joseph never quit believing that God's intentions were meant for good. I want to be that resilient. I want to be that secure. I want to be that certain of God's good intentions. Don't you?

In the previous chapter, I introduced the worksheet tucked into the appendix called "Who *I AM* Is and Who I Am." I mention it again now because I know the pain of allowing anyone apart from God to define me. I can relate to being what Lysa calls "a grabber of people's love." If you can also relate, please consider taking another look at "Who *I AM* Is and Who I Am." Open your hands and heart to receive God's love. Recalling and reciting verses about the character of God and his thoughts for you will empower you to claim your rightful place of belonging and lead you to discover the joy of acceptance.

God's Thoughts Are Not Like Ours

My husband and I have steered our company through several economic turns, but the 2008 recession nearly plunged us over a cliff. I prayed fervently for work and promised God I would walk through any door he opened for me. In my mind, he would answer by sending new business to keep our company from bankruptcy. But God had something else in mind.

Even though I regularly attended a writer's critique group at that time, I didn't think of myself as a writer. Sure, I wrote advertising copy, press releases, and video scripts for marketing and training purposes. I had even self-published a couple of books, but no publishing house had ever offered me a contract, which—in my mind—was a prerequisite to calling oneself a writer.

"You *are* a writer, Shawna." My friend Kim did her best to convince me. "You don't have to be earning royalties as a published author to call yourself a writer."

I didn't believe it.

Then one day at our group, my friend Carrie announced that the regional children's hospital in our community was hiring a full-time writer. I told her she would be perfect for the job and asked if she had applied.

"I don't have a bachelor's." Carrie shrugged. "They require a bachelor's degree to apply."

"Kim, you should apply," I asserted. "You have a degree, right?" She shook her head.

I proceeded to recommend the position to each writer seated around the table. No one had a degree except two retired teachers with no interest in pursuing a new career.

"Huh." I grinned and said with considerable sarcasm, "I guess that means the full-time *writer* job is for me."

As the women gathered around the table laughed, I heard the still, small voice of God: "You are a writer, Shawna. This job *is* for you."

My heart sank. This job opportunity didn't open the door I had in mind. But God's thoughts are not like our thoughts, so I walked through the doorway and landed the job. On my first day, I received my name badge. For security reasons, the hospital didn't include their employees' last names. My first name was centered at the top of the badge, and my title was printed directly beneath it. On several occasions, people addressed me as Shawna Writer.

God's sense of humor makes me giggle. Apparently, he wanted me to identify as a writer. He turned a roadblock to my dreams into a detour that not only polished my writing skills, but also empowered me to believe and speak truth each time someone asked what I did for a living. When I started working at the hospital, I would respond by saying I worked in communications and marketing. I felt comfortable using the same job description I'd given for years. But in time, I began saying, "I'm a writer." Not too long after that, I began believing it.

I memorized Jeremiah 29:11 years ago but discovered a different version of the familiar verse during my season of employment at the children's hospital. The King James Version says, "For I know the thoughts that I think toward you, saith the LORD, thoughts of peace, and not of evil, to give you an expected end."

I must confess, when that scripture came to mind on my morning commute, I'd respond with, "I know *you* know what you're thinking, but *I* can't imagine what you're thinking!" In that season of misunderstanding, I simply had to trust that God knew what he was doing with his way of thinking.

God can give you a future and a hope by merely thinking about you. His thoughts are a done deal. I'm reminded of the saying, "God said it. I believe it. That settles it." However, God doesn't even need to say it. He can simply think it. No wonder Isaiah wrote, "'My thoughts are nothing like your thoughts,' says the LORD. 'And my ways are far beyond anything you could imagine. For just as the heavens are higher than the earth, so my ways are higher than your ways and my thoughts higher than your thoughts'" (Isa. 55:8–9).

What if you accepted that God's thoughts and ways are beyond figuring out? What if you agreed that God's countless thoughts are for you—even when you don't understand his ways? What if you allowed God to set roadblocks and detours to your dreams?

Imagine the impossible lengths God will go to catch you in a trust fall. Declaring God's promises as though they have already transpired demonstrates that you believe God will keep his word—you believe he will do what he says he will do. To be clear, you don't force God to do your will by declaring he is working on your behalf in dire situations. Your act of believing and speaking by faith unleashes the power of God's precious thoughts toward you.

Joseph knew God hadn't forgotten him. In spite of contradicting circumstances, he continued to believe God would keep his promises. I learned that God can use a path that might seem dark and dreary to take me places I never imagined. He will do the same for you. God has a very good reason for teaching us not to lean on our own understanding (see Prov. 3:5–6). Our understanding is limited, but God's thoughts have no limit. God doesn't have to assume. He doesn't even have to presume. He knows the thoughts he thinks toward you, and they are beyond anything your mind can conceive.

Will you dare to believe and speak what no mind can conceive?

God's Thoughts Have No Limit

For ten years, my family traveled to Puerto Vallarta on vacation. We always visited in November because the weather is beautiful and the kids were out of school for Thanksgiving. Once our children were grown and school no longer dictated our time away, I told the family I wanted to visit while the whales were in Banderas Bay. We booked our vacation near the end of whale-watching season, knowing the baby whales born in the bay would be preparing to migrate north with the adults to the feeding grounds.

From the moment our reservations were confirmed, I began asking God for a glorious display of his creation. Every time I told someone we were going to Puerto Vallarta during whale-watching season, I repeated my prayer. *God, you are the sovereign creator. Show me your whales, and I will give you all the glory.* As our vacation neared, I had uttered that prayer so many times that I began telling people the same thing.

"God is the sovereign creator. He has the power to command the whales, so I'm asking him to put on a show, and I promised to give him all the glory."

When we purchased the tickets in Puerto Vallarta, I told the young woman who sold them to us that I had been asking God to show us his whales. She smiled in an encouraging way, and I lifted up a faith-filled prayer right then. The night before our tour, I prayed once more as I climbed into bed. "Tomorrow is the day, God. In Jesus name, I ask you to show me your glorious creation."

God answered by recalling to my mind an extravagance he had given me as a newlywed on a tight budget. The sweet memory came with a promise that Steve and I were about to get the best seats to the best show ever.

The extravagance occurred nearly thirty years ago, shortly after I had learned that Al Jarreau was coming to our hometown to perform. Steve and I had enjoyed listening to his vocal jazz music since before we were married. To make his concert even more enticing, Take 6, a gospel vocal group we also love, would open that memorable event.

"Guess what, Steve!" I remember sharing the news with an abundance of enthusiasm, only to have my husband remind me of our lack of resources.

"This is a chance of a lifetime," I urged. "Have you ever heard of Al Jarreau touring with a gospel group? Let's use our savings."

Steve would not budge. "What if he has an off night?"

"Al Jarreau? Not possible! How could he not be awesome?"

"I'm not spending that kind of money on a couple of tickets if he has an off night." Apparently, Steve had decided the vocalist of the century was going to have pitch problems, and I had to resign myself to missing the greatest show of my life . . . until I saw a chance to win tickets in the newsletter of a local nonprofit agency. I raced to the phone. (Back then, they still hung on walls.)

"I just now read this month's newsletter," I said breathlessly to the woman who answered my call. "I see you're giving away two tickets to the Al Jarreau concert, and today is the last day to enter the drawing." My hope swelled. "No one would be more thrilled to win those tickets than me, but there's no way I can get to your office in time to enter. Will you help me, please? I don't care if you write my name on a napkin. I need to be in that drawing."

The woman agreed, and I thanked her profusely. I hung up and immediately said a prayer. "Oh Lord, I would love to be at that show tomorrow night. May I please have those tickets?"

The woman called back that evening to let me know that I could pick up my winning tickets at will call before the concert. I shared the exciting news with my husband, who is not normally an Eeyore.

"I won the tickets! We've got a date tomorrow night."

"Free tickets from a nonprofit agency?" He frowned. "They will probably be in the far corner of the back row."

Eeyore was outrageously wrong. Our seats were located in the center of the fourth row. The tilt of the theater seating and the height of the stage positioned us perfectly. As we settled in, I proclaimed, "We have the best seats in the house!" The joy of sitting up front was magnified by the phenomenal performances. The opening act brought glory to God as I expected, but the worship continued as Al Jarreau took the stage. He thanked Take 6 for their "invocation" and began praising God with his trademark, freestyle jazz vocals. He proceeded to sing all my favorites flawlessly. The performance exceeded my expectations. As we left the theater, I declared, "We had the best seats to the best show ever!"

As my thoughts drifted back to the present, I knew that God had stirred up this memory to answer my prayer the night before our whale-watching trip. Without a shadow of doubt, I heard him whisper into my heart, "You're about to have the best seats to the best show ever."

The next morning, I told my husband the promise I'd heard from God. "Steve, God is going to put on an amazing show for us today, just like he did with Al Jarreau."

"You think so?"

"I know so!"

Steve nodded. "I think you may be right about that." (Eeyore no more.) His faith encouraged my own.

From that moment, I told anyone who cared to listen that we were about to see an amazing display of God's glorious creation. When I informed the operations manager of the touring company, who greeted us at the dock, I sensed he felt the obligation to moderate my enthusiasm.

"Most people see only a flick of a dorsal fin or maybe a tail," he said. "And regulations keep us from getting too close, but you may get lucky." He held up both hands with crossed fingers.

"We're going to be blessed big time." I grinned. "I've been talking to God, and he promised me we're about to have the best seats to the best show ever." I laugh at the memory of his expressive response. Let's just say, I rendered him speechless.

The next few hours were filled with such a glorious display of God's creation—even the tour guide and boat driver were undone. My husband, who is a professional photographer, took pictures superior to the ones on the company's brochure. I can't even count the number of times we saw whales breaching—baby whales and full-grown males. I acted like a giddy child, clapping my hands, and praising God. The whales gave no regard to the proximity regulations. They danced and spouted a few meters from our little inflatable boat. One lady kept ducking in fear. When she asked the guide if we were safe, I wondered if I should confess, but he assured her the whales wouldn't harm us in any way.

Near the end of our tour, God orchestrated one more opportunity to show off.

"Have you heard of whale song?" the guide asked.

The two dozen or so people filling the little boat all answered affirmatively.

"They don't sing every day, and on the days they do sing, they don't sing all day." He reached for the pole holding the underwater microphone. "But we've been lucky today, so I have a good feeling. Shall we give it a try?"

A chorus of agreement arose. (Although, I knew that luck had nothing to do with it. God was blessing me beyond what I could have imagined.)

The guide submerged the microphone, and as it sloshed into the water, I said, "Father God, make your creatures sing."

As soon as the microphone settled into place, the sound of whale song filled the breezy, ocean air.

"Can you hear that?" The tour guide grinned with shock and awe.

I looked at Steve, and said, "They're singing praises to God." Then I burst into tears.

God is able to do exceedingly more than our minds can conceive. Why put restrictions on our expectations when God's thoughts for us have no limit? An article in *Success* magazine gives this helpful word picture:

> Imagine that you and I are walking down the street.
>
> You breathe in. You breathe out. I breathe in. I breathe out. We both need oxygen to survive. Would you worry that there would not be enough oxygen for both of us? Of course not—air is abundant.
>
> Now imagine we are scuba diving and my scuba tank starts to malfunction. I signal that I need to share the oxygen in your tank. Suddenly the air becomes a precious commodity. Its scarcity makes us worry. What if there isn't enough for both of us?[3]

God doesn't want you to worry that you won't have enough air or enough significance or enough love. Scarcity discounts God's abundant provision. Why nibble on the nonsense that you're not enough when you can feast on the knowledge that you're perfectly proportioned? The morsels of scarcity entice us away from God's banquet of blessings through the temptation to worry. Worry will spoil your appetite, so train your senses to reject its allure. Trade your worries for prayers, and satiate your mouth with thanksgiving. Your trust and gratitude invite inexplicable peace from God. Peace fills the space occupied by worry, and abundance leaves no room for scarcity.

Our finite thought processes must stretch beyond capacity to consider our infinite God. Accepting God's limitless nature goes beyond deciding to look at your cup as half full instead of half empty. Expanding the confines of your mind to make room for the possibilities of God means believing God can cause your cup to overflow no matter its current contents. Anyone who can turn a couple of fish and five loaves of bread into a meal for five thousand men, not even counting the women and children, and end up with twelve baskets of leftovers isn't limited by the supply you see.

I hope your thought processes are evolving. I hope you're learning to reprogram wrong thinking. I hope you're replacing the less-than-precious thoughts you had about yourself with the truth of who God says you are.

Paul's prayer in Ephesians 3:14–21 provides a model for how to pray to the one who can accomplish abundantly beyond what you can imagine—let alone ask for. I love the part that says, "I pray that from his glorious, unlimited resources he will empower you with inner strength through his Spirit."

Will you join me in asking God to do far more for you than you might ask or think? Speak this aloud right now: *Lord, I pray that from your glorious, unlimited resources, you will empower me with inner strength through your Spirit. Amen.*

God loves answering prayers like that because it pleases him to hear you declare your faith in his unlimited resources. Make your request with confidence! Believe God has the means to give you what you ask for. Then, believe him for even more.

What I Thought versus What I Know

We may not understand God's thoughts, but we can trust he knows what he's doing—even when his higher ways don't make any sense. Let's stop assuming the worst and start proclaiming the great things God has in store. Consider what we've learned so far from Psalm 139.

God knows me.

He is always with me.

I am not invisible.

I am wonderfully made.

God's countless thoughts are for me.

I encourage you to believe and speak truth, sister. Declare these five lines from the Manifesto of Acceptance aloud now.

I sincerely believe that demolishing strongholds and taking thoughts captive requires action. That's why I created a second worksheet to build upon the firm foundation you established with the "Who *I AM* Is and Who I Am" exercise. Also found in the appendix, this activity is called "What I Thought versus What I Know," and is designed to spur you out of passivity and into your rightful place of belonging. Complete the activity to call out your destructive thinking patterns and hone your thoughts to align with God's thoughts.

Begin by writing repeated, negative thoughts you have about yourself: *I'm stupid, no one cares about me, my feelings don't matter,* and other lies. Don't worry if your list grows long. God's thoughts outnumber the grains of sand. He has more than enough precious thoughts to come against a legion of lies. And don't worry if the lies are rooted in the painful truth about bad decisions you once made. The details of your past never negate the fact that God's love is unfailing, his mercies unending, and his precious thoughts are undeniably for you—not against you.

Finish by attaching Bible verses to every self-destructive statement. Take your time with this step, and don't feel like you have to tackle every false statement at once. Find verses that confront the lies you allow yourself to think. Contrast the lies about your identity with what God says about the true you. Refer to your "Who *I AM* Is and Who I Am" worksheet to remind yourself what you already know about who you are. Open your Bible for a greater supply of truth. Use a concordance to look up keywords that come to mind or search the Internet for the many promises of God. Once you identify verses with divine power to demolish your specific strongholds, write them alongside the self-destructive statements. As you expose the lies and choose to replace what you once thought with what you now know, your feelings about yourself will come into alignment with how God feels about you. In case you forgot, he's crazy about you! I can hear him singing over you now—no underwater microphone needed.

I encourage you to examine the "What I Thought versus What I Know" worksheet before reading the next chapter. We are about to wage war, but not as the world does. You will need your divinely powered weapons honed and ready to engage in the fight.

Chapter Seven

I HAVE ENEMIES, BUT . . .

Psalm 139:19–22

¹⁹ O God, if only you would destroy the wicked!
Get out of my life, you murderers!
²⁰ They blaspheme you;
your enemies misuse your name.
²¹ O LORD, shouldn't I hate those who hate you?
Shouldn't I despise those who oppose you?
²² Yes, I hate them with total hatred,
for your enemies are my enemies.

I'm sure you've noticed my pattern of opening each chapter with a new set of verses from Psalm 139 and prompting you to read them aloud. I wouldn't blame you if you'd rather not say the verses that set the tone for this chapter. I wouldn't be surprised if you have to spit the words out. Verses 19–22 don't taste the same as the uplifting lyrics David wrote in verses 1–18. Nevertheless, God inspired all Scripture—even David's passionate expression of loathing—to prepare and equip you for life. Like it or not, confronting the enemies of God is a part of life.

Please read Psalm 139:19–22 aloud now if you haven't already.

Jesus taught us to love our enemies, and yet here we are verbalizing total hatred for them. Confusing, right? We can justify David's hatred in light of an important qualifier. Verse 20 says, "your enemies misuse your name," and verse 22 says, "your enemies are my enemies." David is expressing hatred for God's enemies—not people. God's enemies are evil spirits—not flesh and blood. Ephesians 6:12 describes them as evil rulers and authorities of the unseen world, mighty powers in this dark world, and evil spirits in the heavenly places.

We learned back in Chapter Three that David was no stranger to evil spirits. He witnessed the effect they had on King Saul, and he came against them with an unlikely weapon: the music of his lyre. I wonder if David used the same lyre to write the music for Psalm 139.

Up until now, this psalm has poured out praise, which doesn't mean that the previous verses failed to contend against evil spirits. The first five lines of the Manifesto of Acceptance armed us with weapons forged from positive themes in Psalm 139. David's detour from praise and thanksgiving to a sharper-sounding weapon of warfare helps ensure that our Manifesto takes direct aim at evil— which brings us to our next declaration.

I have enemies, but . . .

As a member of the *I'm Special Sisterhood*, you belong to a group of powerful women. We are not victims. We are more than conquerors. Adding the word "but" to the end of our newest declaration hints at our upper hand. Say it aloud to see what I mean.

I have enemies, but . . .

The tongue has the power of life and death. Without the "but," we merely acknowledge the existence of an opposing force. With the addition of this mighty little conjunction, however, we tip the declaration's trajectory toward victory. Say the four-word phrase again—this time with greater emphasis on the triumphant final word.

I have enemies, but . . .

The sword of the Spirit, which is the Word of God, prepares and equips you to stage counterattacks on the enemy of your soul.

Completing the "Who *I AM* Is and Who I Am" worksheet girds you with truth, while the "What I Thought versus What I Know" activity disarms your enemies. With ready access to divinely powered weapons from Scripture and a solid battle plan to demolish strongholds, your victory is assured.

I have enemies, but . . .

Since 1 Peter 5:8 refers to "your great enemy, the devil," I initially considered writing this declaration in the singular form. You and I have an enemy named Satan. Jesus called him a thief and a liar whose purpose is to steal, kill, and destroy. Yes, we have *a* great enemy. However, Satan isn't omnipresent like God. He is a created being that can only be in one place at one time. He has little room in his schedule for personal attacks on the likes of me, but he governs the evil rulers and authorities of the unseen world, the powers in this dark world, and the evil spirits in the heavenly places. Legions of demons under his command perpetrate attacks on ordinary people like you and me. They come after us through all manner of trials and temptations, striking our health, finances, relationships, and more. Sometimes, demonic exploits are disguised as flesh-and-blood adversaries, but we must take these ground wars to the heavenly places. No matter the face of our enemy, we need to fight with spiritual weapons.

The woman known in the New Testament for her hemorrhaging pressed through earthly obstacles for a heavenly touch. She didn't rail against a religious system that forced her into isolation for menstrual bleeding nearly every day of the month. She didn't hire an attorney to file malpractice lawsuits against her costly physicians. She fought for freedom from oppression with faith, courage, and worship. After twelve years of devastating defeat, the woman with constant bleeding gained victory on her knees near the hem of Jesus's garment.

Faith to Shed Shame

You may wonder why I chose to illustrate our enemies with a woman who had a bodily ailment that caused emotional pain. The woman described in Mark 5:25–34 and Luke 8:43–48 didn't encounter opposition from jealous brothers like Joseph or cowardly defectors like Joshua. No flesh-and-blood enemies attacked her physically or harmed her intentionally. However, the faceless foes that struck the woman with constant bleeding are every bit as destructive as the enemies Joseph and Joshua confronted.

You may recognize a few of these enemies: isolation, financial ruin, and shame.

I imagine the woman with constant bleeding heard the Levitical teaching about her "uncleanness" with such frequency she could quote it from memory: "When a woman has a discharge of blood for many days at a time other than her monthly period or has a discharge that continues beyond her period, she will be unclean as long as she has the discharge, just as in the days of her period" (Lev. 15:25 NIV).

The woman's health problem plagued her for twelve years. Her desperate quest for healing drove her to spend everything she had on physicians who caused more harm than good. The failure of these medical treatments essentially severed the woman from her family, friends, and community. The Law of Moses commanded the Israelites to keep separate from things that made them ceremonially unclean. This woman was perpetually unclean.

The constant bleeding that evicted her from the public square also prohibited her from becoming ceremonially clean. Religious requirements called for her to count off seven days after her bleeding stopped, and on the eighth day, present a sin offering and a burnt offering to the priest. She must have anxiously counted consecutive days with no discharge, only to begin flowing again before the end of the week. No eighth-day sacrifice meant no atonement for the uncleanness of her discharge. Stigmatized by a personal health condition that may well have fostered false accusations of a sinful lifestyle, the woman had no hope for redemption through obedience to religious laws.

The woman's enemies of isolation and financial ruin paled in comparison to her dark-red shame.

But shame couldn't keep her from Jesus.

When the woman heard Jesus was in town, she risked her life for the chance to be healed. As detailed in Leviticus 15:25–31, the laws that kept Israelites separate from the things that made them unclean were implemented "so they will not die in their uncleanness for defiling [God's] dwelling place, which is among them." To believe Jesus Christ is the Messiah is to believe he is Emmanuel, God with us. Fully aware she might defile God's dwelling place, the woman pressed into the crowded street to touch Jesus with her unclean hands.

I picture the woman hiding under a headscarf to mask her identity. Anyone recognizing her could expose her uncleanness and send her away from the crowds—away from Jesus. She covertly ventured forth, prepared to break the law, and thought to herself, "If I can just touch his robe, I will be healed."

I could interpret her resolve regarding Jesus's robe in different ways. Did shame lower her expectations from a face-to-face encounter with Jesus to an anonymous tug on his hem? Perhaps she hoped God's anger would be less fierce if she merely grabbed the garment adorning his dwelling place. I'm convinced her daring decision to reach for healing was motivated by faith alone. The drama unfolded as she jostled her way through the crowd, came up behind Jesus, and touched the hem of his garment. At that moment, the woman's bleeding stopped, and she knew she'd been healed.

Though no words were spoken, Jesus knew that healing power had gone out from him. He turned around in the crowd and asked, "Who touched my robe?"

My stomach knots knowing this question toppled our girl from the heights of receiving the healing she desperately sought into a free fall of fear at exposing her blatant disregard for the law.

Luke's version says everyone denied touching Jesus's robe. That means the woman must have denied it too. I picture her quietly shaking her head rather than loudly protesting. Maybe Luke misread her actions. Maybe she shook her head in shock.

Would the crowd rebuke her?

Would Jesus reject her?

Would she die for defiling God's dwelling place?

Peter tried to keep Jesus moving along, saying, "Master, this whole crowd is pressing up against you."

The other disciples agreed, saying, "Look at this crowd pressing around you. How can you ask, 'Who touched me?'"

Jesus would not be dissuaded from connecting with the woman whose faith and courage had invited miraculous healing. He looked around, scanning the crowd. Did he catch her eye? I wouldn't be surprised if she readjusted her headscarf when Jesus said, "Someone deliberately touched me, for I felt healing power go out from me."

Twelve years of bleeding ceased the instant she touched Jesus. Nevertheless, isolation, financial ruin, and shame still assailed her. The fear that kept the woman hiding from Jesus must have convinced her that her suffering hadn't ended with the bleeding. Staying hidden prevented her from complete healing. Rather than allow her faceless foes to keep her in the shadows, the woman came before the Light of the World. Trembling with fright, she fell to her knees in front of Jesus. From her lowly position, she looked up to him. With the whole crowd listening, she confessed her reason for touching, defiling the Son of God. She spoke of her immediate healing, which leads me to believe she also mentioned the nature of her illness.

I imagine her face burned with shame. I can almost hear the whispers of those in the crowd who may have bumped into her. Did their sudden need for ceremonial cleansing anger them? Would they lash out at her? But nothing distracted the woman from making her full confession. Kneeling before Jesus, she surrendered her very existence. This yielded woman offered Jesus a beautifully pure form of worship, and he rewarded her courageous act of faith.

Jesus restored the woman's honor by saying, "Daughter, your faith has made you well. Go in peace. Your suffering is over."

No more isolation because a daughter belongs in the family. No more financial ruin because her faith made her well. No more shame because Jesus ended her suffering. Healed and vindicated by Jesus Christ, the woman known for her constant bleeding could embrace the future with a sense of security and peace.

If the enemies of your body, mind, and spirit have been keeping you in the shadows, it's time to come into the light. You will find the healing you seek by worshipping Jesus. He can turn everything around in an instant with just one touch. To receive his healing, you must press through distractions and come before him. Surrender to your Savior. Allow Jesus to fight your faceless foes. And then, put your enemies on notice by declaring the sixth line in our Manifesto.

I have enemies, but . . .

Sixth Journal Prompt: Psalm 139:19–22

As an avid reader of the Psalms who is trained in the craft of writing, I can't help but notice when David breaks the rules of grammar. Some of his psalms switch between first, second, and third person. For example, Psalm 23 starts out with David writing about the Lord, his shepherd. "He makes me lie down in green pastures, he leads me beside quiet waters, he refreshes my soul."

Midway through the psalm, David begins addressing his shepherd directly. "I will fear no evil, for you are with me; your rod and your staff, they comfort me."

David's inconsistent point of view also appears in Psalm 139:19–20, which bounces between addressing God and addressing the enemies of God. This grammatical faux pas is especially jarring.

O God, if only you would destroy the wicked!
Get out of my life, you murderers!
They blaspheme you; your enemies misuse your name.

Your journaling assignment begins with these two verses and continues through verse 22. Ask God to speak to you, and record what you hear him saying. Consider asking why David abruptly shifted focus with his "Get out" command. After you complete this activity, I will be here to help you suit up with proven weapons for defeating the enemies of God. For now, hold your place with a bookmark, and take time to look, list, learn, listen, and live through Psalm 139:19–22.

Power and Authority to Fight

For decades, I felt uncomfortable holding one of the titles informally given to me. People call me a prayer warrior because I believe in the power of prayer to affect outcomes. I pray when people ask me to and offer to pray when they don't ask. I have seen God move figurative mountains in response to my prayers, but I never felt like a warrior until recently.

Part of my struggle to accept warrior status stemmed from a misunderstanding of spiritual warfare. I did my best to avoid a fight with Satan and his minions. Proverbs 18:10 says, "The name of the LORD is a strong fortress; the godly run to him and are safe." I thought that running to Jesus each time I came under attack made me godly. I prayed Scripture and claimed promises from the shelter of his presence, but I simply hunkered down.

I ran to Jesus to hide.

Then one day, my Savior shocked me. My eyes were closed in prayer. "Protect me, Jesus," I cried. "Save me from this attack." In my mind's eye, I saw myself like a small child peeking out from behind her daddy's knees. I imagined clinging to Jesus's flowing white robes and using him as a shield as I prayed. "Please, Jesus. I need your help." I trusted that he heard my cries and hoped he would answer quickly. "Go get 'em, Lord. Go after my enemies for me." Tucked safely behind Jesus, I retreated into my strong fortress to await rescue.

With my eyes still closed, I saw Jesus turn to me. He shook his head, smiled, and said, "You go get 'em, Shawna. I have given you all power and authority in my name. You go, and I'll be with you."

At that moment, two verses I'd memorized but never internalized surfaced and convicted me. First, I remembered the promise in Luke 10:19 that says, "Look, I have given you authority over all the power of the enemy." Next, a promise from Ephesians 1:19–20 popped into my head. Paul's words to the church at Ephesus came across as if Jesus were speaking directly to me. I heard him say something like, "I pray you understand the incredible greatness of God's power for you. This is the same mighty power that raised me from the dead and seated me in the place of honor at God's right hand in the heavenly realms."

My eyes flew open at the weight of responsibility. I'd been entrusted with the same power God exerted when he raised Jesus Christ from the dead. Could anyone access more power than that? Clearly not! I understood Jesus wasn't telling me that I could no longer run to him. He is my shield and my defender. He always will be. I also understood Jesus's unexpected answer to my prayer was his way of challenging me to walk in authority with the power he had already given me.

I personalized the profound lesson Jesus taught me from his Word and turned it into a truth-infused declaration for anyone who believes God. I challenge you to repeat this declaration aloud until it's internalized—or even memorized:

> God has given me authority over all the power of the enemy. I understand the incredible greatness of God's power for me is the same mighty power that raised Jesus Christ from the dead.

I still prefer to avoid fights with evil spirits, but I no longer automatically run and hide when under attack. I follow David's example and bounce between addressing God and addressing his enemies. I pattern my warrior prayers after Psalm 139, which gives far more attention to God. This balance ensures that I look to God for help while not backing down from contending against the enemies of God when appropriate.

James 4:7–8 also instructs us to contend directly with our enemies while keeping our primary focus on God. The three-step strategy in these verses begins and ends with God:

1. Humble yourselves before God.
2. Resist the devil, and he will flee from you.
3. Come close to God, and God will come close to you.

This resistance must be verbalized. The enemies of God can whisper thoughts into your head, but they can't read your mind. Jesus drove out demons by speaking to them and commanding them to leave. He gave all who believe in him the same power and authority.

If you have not yet declared the verses from Psalm 139 found at the beginning of this chapter, it's not too late. I invite you to revise the last part of verse 19 to substitute "murderers" with another word that helps you more accurately resist your enemies.

"I command you in the name of Jesus Christ. Get out of my life, you _____!"

Fight with Faith

I wish the Bible gave us more of the hemorrhaging woman's story. We don't know what inspired her faith in Jesus. We do know the religious regulations that marked her as unclean, along with the failed medical treatments that drained her finances and robbed her of hope for a normal life. We also know she pursued Jesus with courageous abandon. Refusing to accept defeat, she gained victory through faith, courage, and worship.

The woman with constant bleeding, who is graciously kept anonymous in every New Testament account of her story, has little in common with an Old Testament king. And yet King Jehoshaphat of Judah and Jerusalem demonstrated the same boldness we saw in her story. Jehoshaphat didn't fight with the weapons of the world to rout the armies of Ammon, Moab, and Mount Seir. Like the unnamed woman with constant bleeding, he relied on faith, courage, and worship to gain victory. Since most of 2 Chronicles 20 is dedicated to his story, we can pinpoint the components of his winning strategy. In the face of pending war, Jehoshaphat chose to arm his men with supernatural weapons. His victory lap began by taking a leap of faith.

Terrified by news of the close proximity of the vast army marching against Israel, Jehoshaphat begged the Lord for guidance and ordered everyone in Judah to begin fasting. His prayer as he stood before the community of Judah and Jerusalem is quite telling. Follow the signs to where Jehoshaphat went with his fear.

In fact, take a minute to point to (or underline) every occurrence of the words "you" and "your" in the verses below.

> O Lord, God of our ancestors, you alone are the God who is in heaven. You are ruler of all the kingdoms of the earth. You are powerful and mighty; no one can stand against you! O our God, did you not drive out those who lived in this land when your people Israel arrived? And did you not give this land forever to the descendants of your friend Abraham? Your people settled here and built this Temple to honor your name. They said, "Whenever we are faced with any calamity such as war, plague, or famine, we can come to stand in your presence before this Temple where your name is honored. We can cry out to you to save us, and you will hear us and rescue us."
>
> And now see what the armies of Ammon, Moab, and Mount Seir are doing. You would not let our ancestors invade those nations when Israel left Egypt, so they went around them and did not destroy them. Now see how they reward us! For they have come to throw us out of your land, which you gave us as an inheritance. O our God, won't you stop them? We are powerless against this mighty army that is about to attack us. We do not know what to do, but we are looking to you for help.

Jehoshaphat concentrated on, called on, and counted on God— nineteen times!

Ammon, Moab, and Mount Seir outnumbered Judah three armies to one. Judah's king was justifiably terrified, but he didn't take a census of his kingdom's able-bodied men. He didn't go to the neighboring king of Israel seeking an alliance. He didn't retreat or surrender. Jehoshaphat went straight to God and begged for guidance. Jehoshaphat lifted a prayer that not only acknowledged God's constant protection and provision, but also confessed Judah's inadequacy to conquer a powerful enemy.

The conclusion to Jehoshaphat's prayer demonstrates his willingness to wait on God. "We do not know what to do, but we are looking to you for help." He placed the dire situation in God's hands and left it there. The vast army marching against Jehoshaphat had already reached En-gedi, which is about fifty miles from Jerusalem if they marched up the shoreline of the Dead Sea before heading west but only twenty-five miles away as the crow flies. With certain death and destruction less than a day's journey from Judah's capital city, Jehoshaphat waits with a heart of faith to receive guidance from God.

Faith is a formidable weapon against the powers of darkness. Unlike the weapons of the world, faith holds divine power to demolish strongholds. We've seen how faith prompted Jehoshaphat to seek a supernatural strategy to defeat his enemies. We've seen how faith equipped an outcast to stand up against isolation, financial ruin, and shame. Faith not only invited God's miraculous intervention in Bible times, but faith also equips unlikely warriors like you and me to win modern-day battles—even battles with real bullets. In fact, I once met a man named Willie who is alive today because his wife knew how to fight with faith.

Willie thought his wife had given up on their marriage. She no longer argued with him about his destructive lifestyle. She seemed withdrawn and uncaring. Willie had known only violence and crime his whole life. He was tired of running with the devil, but didn't believe God would accept him. Trapped in a pit of despair, he decided to end his life. He told his wife to take the children and leave the house.

"I was trying to reach out for help," he said to me. "I didn't show it, but I wanted her to stop me."

She didn't stop him. She simply told him to do what he needed to do.

"She kept saying that to me," he said, emotion thick in his throat. "I couldn't believe she didn't try to stop me. She just said, 'Do what you need to do,' and let me walk into the bedroom."

For the next few hours, a battle raged for Willie's soul. He cried out to God but felt overpowered by Satan. Willie attempted suicide again and again.

"I pulled that trigger seven times, and the gun never fired." Willie shook his head and shrugged. My jaw dropped open. "I knew it wasn't jammed because three days prior, I'd shot two rounds. I knew God was saving me, and I told him so."

Tears stung my eyes as I realized his salvation was literal. Jesus saved me from the power of sin and death, but not like he saved Willie.

"That's when I felt love like I've never felt it before," Willie said. "God filled me with so much love. I gave my life to him and told him I was done with my old ways."

When Willie went back into the family room, he found his wife still there.

"I told her what happened and asked why she didn't try to stop me."

I had been wondering the same thing.

"She said she'd been praying to God, asking him what to do." Willie leaned forward in his chair, and I couldn't help but lean in too. "She said God told her not to do anything, that she was supposed to leave me in his hands. That's why she didn't try to stop me that night. That's why she told me to do what I needed to do."

Willie's wife fought the powers of darkness on behalf of her husband through faith. She placed the dire situation in God's hands and left it there. No arguing. No pleading. No calling the police. She looked to God for help, and he answered by transforming Willie's heart and mind.

"God knew that calling the police wouldn't have saved me, and he knew my wife couldn't save me." Willie pointed toward heaven. "He was the only one who could save me, and he did."

Willie's wife witnessed the promise in 1 John 5:4: "For every child of God defeats this evil world, and we achieve this victory through our faith."

Even though sometimes we can't exactly see its mighty power, faith works better than any weapon we could hold in our hands. So let's fight with faith and trust God to bring victory.

Fight with Courage

Fighting with faith takes courage—even with our victory assured. Courage doesn't emerge in the absence of fear. If you think about it, we wouldn't need courage if we weren't afraid. Rather than subtracting fear, we must add faith to the equation.

The correct calculation is Fear + Faith = Courage.

A further look at 2 Chronicles 20 reveals Jehoshaphat's abundant faith and resulting courage. As he waited expectantly for guidance, God spoke clearly through a prophet named Jahaziel. All the men of Judah were standing before the Lord with their wives and little ones when Jahaziel spoke up. The tension permeating the atmosphere must have been every bit as intense as the day Willie's wife and children stood by while he held a gun to his head. Please don't think the supernatural activity that happened in biblical times can't happen today. A perfectly functioning gun that doesn't fire is every bit as miraculous as a prophet who suddenly declares, "Listen! This is what the LORD says."

After declaring those words, Jahaziel brought this message from God: "Do not be afraid! Don't be discouraged by this mighty army, for the battle is not yours, but God's."

Jahaziel's prophetic word assured Jehoshaphat's army they wouldn't even need to fight. "Take your positions; then stand still and watch the LORD's victory. He is with you, O people of Judah and Jerusalem. Do not be afraid or discouraged. Go out against them tomorrow, for the LORD is with you!"

Jehoshaphat led his army out early the next morning, full of faith and courage. He stopped in the wilderness on the way to war and said, "Listen to me, all you people of Judah and Jerusalem! Believe in the LORD your God, and you will be able to stand firm. Believe in his prophets, and you will succeed."

Jehoshaphat gave more than a pep talk the morning Judah marched against its enemies. I say similar words to you right now: *Listen to me, all you members of the* I'm Special Sisterhood! *Believe in the Lord your God, and you will be able to stand firm. Believe you can hear God speak, and you will succeed.*

I would never call a step in our journaling activity "listen" if I didn't believe God still speaks today. I can't tell you how he will speak to you—only that he will. Tragically, the enemy speaks too, and while his hateful, condemning voice sounds nothing like our loving God, he is a master of disguise. If you find yourself retreating in fear from what you hear, I promise you aren't hearing from God.

I learned to discern my Father's voice from my enemy's when Scott was a toddler. My routine as a young mom was to drop my daughter at school, take my son to his daycare provider, and then spend time in prayer and Bible reading before beginning my workday. One morning during my usual prayer time, a clear, distinct thought popped into my head.

"Why haven't you dedicated your son to me?"

I immediately assumed that I had heard the voice of God, but I didn't want to talk to him about a baby dedication ceremony for

Scott. I cut my prayer time short and turned my attention to business. The next morning, I heard it again.

"Why haven't you dedicated your son to me?"

Anxiety gripped me. As I had done the day before, I closed my Bible and opened my work folder. The disturbing question lingered in my mind all morning. The next day, I heard the same voice invade my Bible reading and prayer time, but the question turned into a sharp command.

"Why haven't you dedicated your son to me? Give him to me. He is mine. You must give him to me."

Guilt pounded through my chest, followed by a hint of anger. Scott brought joy to my aching heart after Sam died. He was mine. I had no desire to get up on the platform at my church for a baby dedication ceremony and causally hand him over to God. I had willingly dedicated my daughter to the Lord when she was three months old, but Sam had been ripped from my arms before he turned three weeks old.

"No," I whispered. "I'm not ready."

But that didn't end it. The voice began haunting me. I honestly don't remember how many of my mornings with God were cut short by this unwelcome exchange, but I do remember the last day it happened. That particular morning, the voice that popped into my head during prayer time said, "Give Scott to me. You know he is mine. If you don't give him to me, I'll take him like I took Sam."

Fear invaded my entire being, and I began to weep. "No, God. Please, no."

"Obey me or your son is going to die." The voice was unrelenting.

I threw myself on the floor, prostrate before God. "You already took Sam. I can't let you take Scott too." I choked out the words, my face soaked with tears. "Please, God. Don't ask me to do this." Lying face down on the carpet before God made something come alive in my terrified spirit. "Help me, God," I sobbed. "You gave your son for me. I want to be able to give my son to you, but I can't. I've heard you asking me to dedicate Scott, but I can't lose another child." Only a few times in my life have I cried out so desperately. My stomach felt nauseous, and my heart felt hollow.

In that moment of honest brokenness before God, a blanket of peace fell over me. A gentle voice whispered softly into my thoughts. "That wasn't me."

The voice sounded the same in terms of being a thought popping into my head, like when I talk to myself. But it was altogether different in tone.

"What?"

"That wasn't me."

"It wasn't? All this time, that wasn't you?" My confusion, like fog, began lifting.

With great compassion, God continued to speak the truth in love. He helped me to see that as long as I had harbored a spirit of rebellion, he allowed me to be deceived. But the moment I came to him with a desire to obey, he revealed his presence.

Fear dissipated and hope flooded my battered soul, along with a strong resolve to never turn away from God out of fear. To be perfectly honest, this painful lesson not only taught me to discern the voice of God; it also multiplied my understanding of why David hated God's enemies with total hatred. I will never again allow Satan to deceive me through willful rebellion against God. I will never again retreat in fear from what I believe God is telling me. By God's grace, I will add faith to my fear and press on with the courage that God gives.

God doesn't want us to be afraid. Retreating in fear gives the enemy opportunities to creep in. Fear scares us into giving up ground that is rightfully ours. God wants us to stand in faith, not retreat in fear. Jehoshaphat didn't stand down, even after Jahaziel said, "The battle is not yours, but God's." Instead of heaving a big sigh of relief and dismissing everyone to their homes, Jehoshaphat obeyed God's instructions to march against the enemy. He and his army took their positions, stood still, and watched the Lord's victory.

Back in Chapter Five, I ended the Tale of the Warm Fuzzies with a veiled warning that the wicked sorceress hadn't been entirely defeated—just put off for a season. In the same way, our enemy waits for an opportune time to attack. He knows our vulnerabilities. That's why he came after me about dedicating Scott. When I walked through the valley of the shadow of my son Sam's death without adding faith to my fear, evil nearly crushed me. But when I trusted the Lord my Shepherd with my deepest longings, he restored my soul. In the midst of that nightmare of deception and rebellion, I found the courage to obey by clinging to God's love for me.

After I opened up with God about my reluctance to dedicate my son, he filled me with such peace that I signed up for the next available baby dedication. I remember the pastor calling all the families participating in the Sunday morning ceremony to come onto the platform. Several young families approached, cradling their tiny infants. Steve and I joined them with our toddler in tow. The memory of that peculiar scene warms my heart. It stands as a reminder to add faith to my fear, and summon the resulting courage to stand and watch the Lord's victory.

No matter who or what frightens you, God is greater. So increase your faith, sister. Courage is the sum of a simple—yet demanding—equation: Fear + Faith = Courage.

Fight with Worship

Back in my twenties, my church introduced a Sunday school class on spiritual warfare. The topic intrigued me, as did the fact that the teacher had belonged to a satanic cult prior to completing seminary and entering vocational Christian ministry. He held a unique angle as one who had stood on both sides of the battlefield.

I arrived the first day of class to find an unassuming man with a big smile on his face and a guitar in his lap. I also found folding chairs placed into a large circle rather than in lecture-style rows. The unexpected classroom configuration set the stage for a greater surprise.

I sat directly across from the teacher, ready to learn. He began right on time by saying his name and nothing more. He then led the class in a familiar old hymn accompanied by his guitar, and followed with a few praise and worship choruses. I expected his teaching to begin after the music stopped, but instead, he proclaimed Scripture, thanked and praised God, and began another set of music. The unquestioning class members sang along. Was I the only one who noticed that half the time allotted for our class had ticked away? When the teacher stopped strumming his guitar a second time, he read a Psalm, invited several in attendance to read portions of Scripture and more Psalms, and then he prayed for God's blessing and power.

We sang another chorus.

I glanced at my watch and shifted in my folding chair. I tried to make eye contact with the teacher so I could express my confusion. And impatience. Did he forget to prepare a lesson? Didn't he know he was wasting precious time? When would he get down to business?

Finally, the teacher set his guitar aside and rose to his feet. I will never forget the words he used to dismiss the class.

"You've come to learn about spiritual warfare, and that's exactly what we've engaged in for the past hour." He didn't look like a mighty warrior, but he exuded strong confidence as he said, "We'll learn more in the weeks to come, but today we wielded our best weapon against our enemy. We worshiped God in spirit and truth."

Jehoshaphat also fought with worship. His winning strategy stationed singers—armed with only their voices—closer to the advancing enemy than Judah's fighting men. The singers' lyrics had nothing to do with war. They sang, "Give thanks to the LORD; his faithful love endures forever!"

As soon as the singers stirred the atmosphere with praise, the Lord caused confusion among the enemy armies. First, Moab and Ammon killed their allies from Mount Seir, and then they turned on each other. By the time Judah's army ascended to the lookout point, every single enemy soldier had been struck down and lay motionless among vast amounts of equipment and other valuables to plunder. After three days of hauling off as much as they could carry, the people of Judah marched victoriously into Jerusalem to the music of harps, lyres, and trumpets.

Jehoshaphat's winning strategy to fight with worship deterred future conflicts as effectively as it defeated current foes. Upon hearing that the Lord himself had fought for Judah, all the surrounding kingdoms shrank back in fear and left God's people in peace. Worshiping God might be our last inclination in the heat of battle, but Jehoshaphat proved that this strategy works. Like the singers on the front lines of Judah's pending war, we can confidently march against our enemies armed only with the instruments of praise—as long as we're wearing the whole armor of God.

Ephesians 6:13–17 details each piece of armor God provides to ensure victory. The divine items include:

1. Belt of truth
2. Breastplate of righteousness
3. Shoes of readiness given by the gospel of peace

4. Shield of faith
5. Helmet of salvation
6. Sword of the Spirit (Word of God)

When I attended the Sunday school class on spiritual warfare, I learned to put on the whole armor of God—not just certain pieces. At the time, I could run away in my gospel shoes, duck under my helmet of salvation, and quench a few flaming arrows with my shield of faith. However, I spent little time reading the Bible and communing with God in prayer, and I confined my worship to once every Sunday. With my belt of truth slacking, I fell for lies. With my breastplate of righteousness loose, I slipped into sin. With no sword of the Spirit in my hand, I entered the battlefield defenseless.

Satan's primary motivation behind every attack is to keep you from worshiping God. When a battle is raging, you may not feel like giving God praise, glory, and honor. Hesitancy to bow before God and look to him for a solution might stem from believing two popular lies:

1. God helps those who help themselves.
2. God never gives you more than you can bear.

Have you heard these lies before? Both are attributed to Scripture, but you won't find these wrong beliefs in either the Old Testament or the New Testament—especially the first one. Nothing close to "God helps those who help themselves" appears anywhere in the Bible.

Jehoshaphat cried out, "We do not know what to do, but we are looking to you for help." He gained a miraculous victory as a result. The woman with constant bleeding thought, "If I can just touch his robe, I will be healed." Her dependence on God brought instant healing to her body. Believing the lie that you should help yourself keeps the focus on you and what you can do. The first lie suggests that God is looking to you and requiring something of you. Operating from the perspective that your success is up to you sounds more like idolatry than worship. Worshipers exalt God and humble themselves.

The second lie distorts truth by misrepresenting part of a Bible verse. Take a look at this verse in context. I bolded the part that's been twisted into a popular lie:

> So, if you think you are standing firm, be careful that you don't fall! No temptation has overtaken you except what is common to mankind. **And God is faithful; he will not let you be tempted beyond what you can bear**. But when you are tempted, he will also provide a way out so that you can endure it. Therefore, my dear friends, flee from idolatry. (1 Cor. 10:12–14 NIV)

These verses promise God will provide a way out when you're tempted and caution you from thinking too highly of yourself— quite the opposite of the second lie. Assuming that you should be strong enough to bear whatever hardship comes your way sets unrealistic expectations about your abilities. Paul authored the oft-misrepresented verse, and he would never agree with the lie that God won't allow you to suffer more than you can handle. In fact, his second letter to the Corinthians states the opposite:

> We think you ought to know, dear brothers and sisters, about the trouble we went through in the province of Asia. We were crushed and overwhelmed beyond our ability to endure, and we thought we would never live through it. In fact, we expected to die. But as a result, we stopped relying on ourselves and learned to rely only on God, who raises the dead. (2 Cor. 1:8–9)

To fight with worship means to rely entirely on God. No need to help yourself as a condition to receive God's help. No false sense of security or bravado that you can handle whatever comes your way. Worship exalts God and humbles the worshiper.

Having nursed my children through a sufficient number of cold and flu bugs by the time my youngest reached kindergarten, I thought I had seen it all—until the night my six-year-old son ran into my darkened bedroom sobbing. I immediately smelled the stomach-churning clue to why he had interrupted my sleep and hurried him into the bathroom. My husband took charge of comforting Scott while his tiny tummy continued to empty its contents. I headed to Scott's room to tackle the expected cleanup job. I remember saying a prayer as I walked down the hall, asking God for healing for my son as well as a quick return to sleep. I needed rest before an early morning flight scheduled to take me to a women's retreat the next day. I had been invited to speak the following night, three times the day after, and once the day after that. I flicked the light switch to my son's bedroom, and dropped my jaw in shock. To this day, I have no idea how he could've made such a huge mess from such a tiny tummy.

"What. Is. This?" I spoke into the empty room.

Immediately, my flesh grew cold, and I heard a voice in my head. "This is a spiritual attack."

No need to discern where that eerie voice came from; I knew from the hair standing up on the back of my neck. My enemy wanted to keep me from ministering that weekend.

"OK, then," I spoke with a confidence I didn't feel. "Then, glory to God. He is worthy to be praised." My voice shook with fear. I summoned all the faith I could muster and began singing the first worship chorus that came to mind. I continued singing and praising God out loud as I stripped the bed, washed the walls, cleaned the carpet, and put Scott's soiled pajamas in the washing machine with the sheets. Then with whispered prayers of thanks-giving, I plucked my little guy from sleeping soundly next to his dad and tucked him under fresh sheets in his room.

I lowered my exhausted body into bed knowing God was about to do amazing things at the women's retreat that weekend. He did not disappoint. His Spirit worked through me mightily, bringing salvation and igniting hope. I could've flown home with-out an airplane.

My husband had assured me by phone that our son showed no signs of illness the morning I left town and had been the pic-ture of health ever since. The moment I arrived home, Scott ran out to greet me in the driveway. He twirled and danced around the car with youthful energy as Steve unloaded my suitcase from the trunk.

"I'm glad to see you are feeling better." I gave Scott a big hug. "It was hard leaving you last Friday when you were so sick."

"I'm all better now, Mommy," he said.

"So, how was the retreat?" my husband asked. "I figure it must have been awesome based on what happened Thursday night."

I launched into a recap of the highlights but grew distracted by Scott.

"Take that!" he demanded as he stomped his foot on the concrete driveway. "Go back down where you belong, devil." He pounded the ground by jumping on the invisible portal.

"What are you doing, Scott?"

"I know who made me sick." Scott used his foot to smack the concrete again.

I looked at Steve. He read my questioning eyes and shook his head. "I didn't say anything to him."

"Who made you sick?"

"The little devil who was dancing and laughing in my room."

My heart missed a beat and then caught up with a thud to my chest. "You saw a devil in your room?"

Scott nodded without a hint of fear. "Yes, but Jesus made him go away."

I watched Scott skip back into the house oblivious to the fact that he had set my heart to pounding. Thankfully, nothing like that eerie attack happened in our home again. That surreal encounter with my enemy seared into my soul the power of worship as a spiritual weapon. It also prompted me to become more proactive in preempting future attacks through prayer. In fact, I contacted my prayer team before I began writing this chapter, asking for additional prayer cover. The Lord faithfully answered by providing the strength and protection I needed. You and I are woefully ill equipped to defeat the powers of hell on our own, but we are not on our own. We belong to God, and he has given us all power and authority to fight and conquer our enemies.

God sent his Spirit to live in you the moment you received his Son as Savior and Lord. Far greater than the spirit who lives in this world, the Spirit within you has already secured your victory. When you come under attack, worship God. If you don't know what to say or do, try lifting the battle cry of Jehoshaphat's army: "Give thanks to the LORD; his faithful love endures forever!" In the heat of the battle, take time to thank God for your assured victory. The enemy can't stand the sound of your praises—especially when they rise above heart-pounding fear.

I have enemies, but . . .

With access to divinely powered weapons to demolish strongholds, I can walk in victory!

Chapter Eight

I CAN WALK IN VICTORY!

Psalm 139:23–24

²³ Search me, O God, and know my heart;
test me and know my anxious thoughts.
²⁴ Point out anything in me that offends you,
and lead me along the path of everlasting life.

With the last two verses of Psalm 139, David lifts a prayer. His request is short but deep. And dangerous.

Asking God to bring on trials that reveal hidden anxieties takes guts. Asking him to stir up your conscience to expose offenses takes humility. Asking him to direct your path takes a willingness to surrender.

By God's grace, David was courageous, humble, and yielded to the will of God. The same measure of grace is available to you, so be bold! Make David's prayer your own. Speak Psalm 139:23–24 out loud now.

The path of everlasting life not only arrives at a heavenly destination; it also meanders across earthly landscapes. At various points along the way, the path inevitably winds through a quiet meadow, scales a rocky mountainside, or descends into a shadowy valley. No matter the terrain, the path of everlasting life is paved with hope. It leads sojourners into promised territory mapped out for you in the last line of the Manifesto.

I can walk in victory!

I don't know where the path of everlasting life has taken you, but I do know you have never traveled it alone. God has been present with you every step of the way. For this reason, you can declare the last line of the Manifesto of Acceptance with confidence.

I can walk in victory!

Regardless of how you feel or act on any given day, you can walk in victory every single day. God has given you all power and authority to live as an overcomer. Will you? That's up to you. Simply because you *can* walk in victory doesn't mean you *will*. My deliberate choice of the word "can" ensures that our newest declaration fills your mouth with truth, which has been my goal from page one. All seven lines of the Manifesto are true.

God knows me.

He is always with me.

I am not invisible.

I am wonderfully made.

God's countless thoughts are for me.

I have enemies, but . . .

I can walk in victory.

You have my permission to take the final declaration one step further by saying, "I can *and will* walk in victory." You have the freedom to decide whether to walk in victory or retreat in defeat. Nothing and no one can keep a child of God from victorious living. Not your friends and family. Not your circumstances. Not your past.

Declare your ability to overcome. Please, speak our final declaration aloud now.

I can walk in victory!

Since the tongue has the power of life and death, semantics matter. To wholeheartedly believe and speak of your ability *and will* to walk in victory, you must have a clear picture of what victory looks like. Living victoriously doesn't mean you never face defeat. Just look at the example of the apostle Paul—or any of the biblical characters sketched in this book. Those who walk in victory don't trip and fall over setbacks. They don't identify as victims or even as survivors. They identify as overcomers and more than conquerors. Rather than allowing momentary battles to ransack their hopes for the future, those who walk in victory maintain an eternal perspective.

In my humble opinion, Paul mastered the art of walking through the wall of defeat into the halls of victory better than anyone—other than Jesus, of course. From the woman at the well to the woman with constant bleeding, along with all the biblical characters I've sketched in between, no one better illustrates walking in victory than Paul. Adopting his view of victorious living may help you gain God's perspective concerning your own wins and losses.

What Victory Looks Like

If Paul's life were a game of baseball, no umpire could deter him by shouting, "You're out!" No booing crowd could keep him from coming out swinging. No fouls or flies could stop him from sliding into home. Paul's preaching seemed to cause more riots than revivals, but he listened to the cheers of heaven rather than the jeers of men. He focused on making marks of eternal significance rather than gaining fifteen minutes of fame. Paul boasted about bizarre things like being in prison more frequently and being flogged more severely than other servants of Christ. He celebrated wins that looked like losses, such as being exposed to death again and again.

Paul wrote this list of "boasts" in 2 Corinthians 11:24–27:

Five times I received from the Jews the forty lashes minus one. Three times I was beaten with rods, once I was pelted with stones, three times I was shipwrecked, I spent a night and a day in the open sea, I have been constantly on the move. I have been in danger from rivers, in danger from bandits, in danger from my fellow Jews, in danger from Gentiles; in danger in the city, in danger in the country, in danger at sea; and in danger from false believers. I have labored and toiled and have often gone without sleep; I have known hunger and thirst and have often gone without food; I have been cold and naked. (NIV)

That doesn't look like a list of wins to me, but Paul was willing to endure anything if it would help bring people to Jesus. After yet another shipwreck, Paul ended up on the island of Malta (Acts 28:1–9 NIV). The islanders built a fire to take the bite off the cold, rainy weather, and Paul helped gather firewood. Apparently, one of the sticks turned out to be a poisonous snake. It bit Paul, who had not only just survived a life-threatening storm at sea but also managed to avoid execution by soldiers who feared his escape.

After witnessing the snakebite, the islanders figured that Paul must have been the worst kind of fugitive. They said, "This man must be a murderer; for though he escaped from the sea, the goddess Justice has not allowed him to live." But Paul merely shook off the snake attached by its fangs to his hand into the fire. The islanders expected him to die or at least swell up badly from the bite. Neither happened, so they decided he was a god instead.

I can't help but grin. Paul went from suspected murderer to supposed god. None of that would've happened if he hadn't been shipwrecked or bitten. While on the island, Paul prayed for the sick people who lived there. All were cured. Victory!

Paul undoubtedly praised God for the miraculous healings that took place on Malta. Based on his list of boasts detailed above, I'm guessing he also praised God for the shipwreck and snakebite. In his letter to the Philippians, Paul indicated he didn't know which he preferred: living through beatings, imprisonment, and other calamities to continue his fruitful work for Christ, or dying so he could go and be with Jesus in heaven. At the time, he thought it best to continue living for the sake of those who benefitted from his ministry. He expressed a different longing a few years later.

Near the end of his life, Paul must have reflected on the rocky, thirty-something years of breaking ground with the gospel—from his dramatic conversion to Christianity to his final days awaiting execution for his faith. I picture Paul relieved and expectant as he wrote in 2 Timothy 4:7, "I have fought the good fight, I have finished the race, and I have remained faithful." In verse 18 of Paul's second letter to Timothy—quite possibly his last letter—he wrote, "Yes, and the Lord will deliver me from every evil attack and will bring me safely into his heavenly Kingdom. All glory to God forever and ever! Amen."

So be it. Paul knew that being rescued didn't necessarily mean staying alive. He explained why in 1 Corinthians 15:51 and 53:

> But let me reveal to you a wonderful secret. We will not all die, but we will all be transformed!
> . . . For our dying bodies must be transformed into bodies that will never die; our mortal bodies must be transformed into immortal bodies.

I wouldn't be surprised if Paul longed for that kind of transformation—especially in light of his many persecutions. He knew death had been swallowed up in victory when Jesus Christ rose from the dead, and he wasn't afraid to die. Paul expected to receive the crown of righteousness as a prize for fighting and finishing well. He knew nothing and no one could take this crown from him—not in life, not in death.

The same prize awaits you.

The righteous Judge canceled the debt of your sin the minute you received Jesus Christ as Lord and Savior. You can walk in victory—in life *and* in death—because Jesus died to break the power of sin, which Paul called "the sting that results in death" (1 Cor. 15:56). Sin lost its power over you when you were "crucified" with Christ—when you received the forgiveness Jesus purchased for you on the cross. "Dying" with Christ set you free from the power of sin. This "death" ensures eternal life with Christ. That's why Paul wasn't afraid to die *and* why he wasn't afraid to live. Paul boasted about his hardships to show us that victory can look more like shipwrecks and snakebites than the miracles of Malta. Walking in victory requires an eternal perspective with eyes fixed on a heavenly prize.

Your prize awaits you, sister.

If you're ready to rise above setbacks, upsets, even landslide defeats, then you have a choice to make. Because of what Jesus Christ has done for you, you can walk victoriously as more than a conqueror.

Will you?

Will you choose Paul's counterintuitive approach to assessing losses?

Will you choose to receive the victory God offers as a gift of love?

Jesus sees you for the champion you are. You simply must choose to overcome by faith. Even if you lack resolve or don't have the strength, Jesus stands ready to tip the scales in your favor. Even with a handicap, you can come out on top. So declare your ability to win now.

I can walk in victory!

Seventh Journal Prompt: Psalm 139:23–24

I am incredibly proud of you for accepting the challenge to journal through Psalm 139. Your faithfulness has equipped you with supernatural keys to break free from the trap of wrong thinking and wrong standing. As you sort through the keys you've been collecting from the twenty-four verses in Psalm 139, God will reveal your unique set of truths with keys to lock out lies about your worthiness to belong and be loved, and keys to unlock the power and authority you already have within you as a child of God.

If you've taken the deeper dive into completing the worksheets presented in the appendix, then you've acquired additional keys to freedom. Designed to help you renounce lies and cancel their negative effects by believing and speaking truth, these worksheets reinforce your true identity and great worth. The Bible verses and declarations on the worksheets have fortified you with mighty weapons to fight against the powers of darkness. Everything you need to claim your rightful place of belonging is within your grasp.

I invite you to revisit your journal one more time. As you work your way through the last two verses of Psalm 139, listen closely to how God answers your prayer to be searched and exposed. Allow him to be honest with you about what he sees in your heart. At the same time, carefully discern the voice of your loving Heavenly Father. Refuse to accept the deceiver's lies.

You'll need that bookmark at least once more as you temporarily redirect your attention from this book to your journal. When you return, I will lead you a few more steps toward discovering the joy of acceptance.

Step Out of Rejection

A few years ago, my mother called me because her computer kept crashing.

"I think it might be the new security system that guy installed," she said.

"What security system?" My internal alarm sounded. My aging mother, who regularly confessed her feelings of confusion, no longer made important decisions without a family discussion.

"I think it's something like what your dad used to install when he was alive. I wish he were still here. . . ."

Her voice drifted off, but I pulled her back with an increasing sense of concern. "Mom, how did you install the security system?"

"I got a phone call from some guy who sold it to me and directed me how to download it onto my computer."

My pulse raced, but I forced calm into my voice. "Do you know how to disconnect your computer from the internet?"

"I think so."

"Please do that right now, and I'll come by to get your computer as soon as I can."

We exchanged good-byes, and I hung up. With phone still in hand, I took immediate measures to protect my mother's stolen identity. Fortunately, the credit card company credited the scam purchase and issued a new card, the Social Security Administration locked down her account, and her bank transferred her assets into a new account with little time and effort.

However, Mom's computer required major servicing. Infected with several strands of malware, the hard drive had to be completely erased and a new operating system installed.

Our brains function like sophisticated hard drives, and rejection impairs proper function like malware. The world may con us into buying its false brand of security, but only God keeps us safe from identity theft.

I hope you don't hate me for telling you this, but, sadly, there is no cure for rejection. Nothing this side of heaven will inoculate you from being left out, overlooked, or disregarded.

Not long ago, I learned about a birthday party attended by a handful of my closest girlfriends honoring someone I consider a friend. I felt the sting of missing out on the fun and—more to the point—being uninvited. These painful moments trigger flare-ups of my chronic rejection disease. But now I have the remedy to relieve the aching symptoms and can send that illness into remission.

As Dr. Guy Winch writes,

> We all have a fundamental need to belong to a group. When we get rejected, this need becomes destabilized and the disconnection we feel adds to our emotional pain. Reconnecting with those who love us, or reaching out to members of groups to which we feel strong affinity and who value and accept us, has been found to soothe emotional pain after a rejection.[1]

I took a quick detour on my way to the first gathering of my writers' critique group after I landed the publishing contract that led to this book, stopping at the grocery store for a bottle of sparkling apple cider. Hugs and high fives from my writing friends greeted me upon arriving at our usual spot. When I set champagne flutes and the bottle of bubbly on the table, Kim made an observation that gave me a second reason to celebrate.

"I love how *you* brought this for us to toast *you*," she said, wearing the same grin she used to encourage me each time she called me a writer when I didn't believe it. "Our younger selves would've wondered if anyone would do this for us and secretly hoped they would, but now that we're older we do it for ourselves."

I raised my glass to toast my victory. The older (and wiser) me had stepped out of a rejection mindset. *I* deserved to be celebrated, so *I* bought the bubbly!

Don't underestimate the value of victory celebrations. They help us better sustain our losses. We often discover the joy of acceptance only to have a rejection roll in and bury it. We grab hold of the assurance that we belong only to lose our grip when a friend blows us off. We stand tall on truth only to wobble when lies knock us backward.

No amount of willpower or positive thinking can help us step out of the rejection mindset to walk in complete victory. We achieve victory through our faith in Jesus. He overcame the world, and anyone who believes he is the Son of God can be an overcomer too.

If you haven't surrendered your life to Jesus Christ, if you haven't asked him to forgive your sins, if you haven't invited him to be your Lord and Savior, take your first step onto the path of everlasting life. To begin a new life in Christ, openly declare this now: *I believe in you, Jesus! I believe you are my Lord, the Son of God. I believe in my heart God raised you from the dead. I believe you came to save me and give me eternal life. I believe!*

Making this confession for the first time takes courage. No one needs courage to retreat. Adding faith to fear gives you the courage to take action. The previous chapter contained an equation for courage. Here's one for victory: Courage + Action = Victory.

Step into Action

From the very start of this book, I've been repeating two action steps: believe and speak. I provided Biblical references to support the efficacy of this practice—from an ancient proverb about the power of the tongue to Old Testament chronicles and New Testament lessons on the transformative power of faith. I gave examples of this believe-and-speak practice bearing fruit—from beckoning whales to leap out of the sea to chasing a little devil out of my son's bedroom. I called you to believe and speak—from learning our secret signal to declaring our seven-line Manifesto. I hope you are well practiced at taking these two action steps. Your longing to belong will be satisfied when you believe the truth spelled out in Psalm 139 and speak what you know to be true.

The call to action in this book is based on 2 Corinthians 4:13–14:

> It is written: "I believed; therefore I have spoken." Since we have that same spirit of faith, we also believe and therefore speak, because we know that the one who raised the Lord Jesus from the dead will also raise us with Jesus and present us with you to himself. (NIV)

Did you know that you have the same spirit of faith as the author of Psalm 139 and the author of 2 Corinthians? Did you know that you have the same spirit of faith as the woman at the well and the woman with constant bleeding? That spirit of faith guarantees the ultimate victory: being raised with Jesus and presented to God himself.

Believing truth is the first step toward discovering the joy of acceptance. Think about what you're thinking about, and make sure your thoughts align with God's Word. Agree with God about who you are and who he is. Trust him to guide you along the path of everlasting life to certain victory.

Speaking life is the second step toward discovering the joy of acceptance. Your words and actions reinforce what you believe. Strip your tongue of the power of death by renouncing any lies you've believed. Cancel the lasting negative effects of those lies by infusing your tongue with the power of life from Scripture.

One fateful evening, while making calls for my church, I cringed to watch the oppressive snare of a lying tongue squelch the joy of a woman we visited. I rang her doorbell and waited on the porch with two other members of our team. Before the woman had fully opened the door, an angry voice blasted her from behind: "You get the door! I'm watching TV!"

"I got it," she called over her shoulder, which appeared to be holding the weight of an arduous relationship.

I put on my brightest smile as I introduced the team and myself. "You came to visit us last Sunday, and we wanted to return the blessing and come visit you."

"Who's there?" the man shouted from the other room. His slurred speech and agitation suggested he might have been drinking.

"It's just some people from church."

"Church?" He laughed with no mirth, only mocking.

The low odds of being invited inside were all that kept me from running away.

"He doesn't want me going to church." Her confession made me grateful the angry man chose laughter over an altogether different reaction to our presence on his porch.

I asked if she had any questions about our church. She said no.

I asked if she knew for certain she would go to heaven. Rarely did I receive a negative response to this question. Pretty much everybody thinks they are going to heaven. But not this woman.

"I won't be in heaven," she said, shaking her head sadly.

My heart broke.

The man yelled again. "You still at the door with those people?"

"Give me a minute," she called back, with only the slightest hint of frustration.

"Let's suppose you could stand before God in heaven," I said. "If he asked you why he should let you in, what would you say?"

"I would tell him I don't deserve to be let in, but that Jesus died for me, and since Jesus covered my sins with his blood, I've been forgiven."

"You believe that?" I asked.

She nodded. "I asked Jesus to be my Lord and Savior when I was a little girl. I never stopped believing."

"But that means you *will* be in heaven." This woman puzzled me. She answered the first question "No" when most answered "Yes," and she answered the second question correctly when most wrongly reason that their own good works and morality will get them into heaven.

"When you put your faith in Jesus, you receive the gift of eternal life by God's grace." I assured her.

She shook her head. "No, I've made too many mistakes."

"But—"

"You still at the damn door?" The man's anger cut me off and spooked all four of us on the porch.

"I'd better go." The woman started to close the door but held it open just a crack. "Thank you," she said.

"I hope you'll come back this Sunday." I had never said anything truer in my life.

"I'll try," she said.

The door closed, and I never saw her again.

To this day, I wish I'd had more time with her to help her acknowledge the truth of who she is because of Jesus—redeemed and delivered, blameless and spotless, deeply loved and precious, and worthy of spending eternity in heaven. Sadly, she believed Satan's lie that she'd made too many mistakes. Even though she'd received eternal life and all the spiritual blessings of being united with Christ, she didn't walk in freedom. While saved from the fires of hell, she lived light-years from enjoying heaven on earth.

Discovering the joy of acceptance begins with two primary action steps: believing truth and speaking life. The resulting journey includes two additional steps: identifying and renouncing lies. When I hear negative self-talk spreading nonsense through my head, I stop to consider the origin of those destructive thoughts.

I've made a habit of asking myself what lies I currently believe. Sometimes I need the help of an honest friend—like the one who set me straight at a photo shoot to promote our fall Bible study series with the teaching team from my church. Andi could see pain behind my forced smile and sought me out later.

"You weren't yourself yesterday," she said. "Something was bothering you. What was it?"

Andi happens to reach the same height as my college roommates. She stood in the center of our photo, where the tall people stand. I was out on the far end, where the short people stand.

"Was I that obvious?" Hadn't I conquered the shorter-than-equals-less-than lie by now? Clearly, I needed to break free—again.

"Only to me."

My secret mostly safe, I could try to slink away in my chains, but conviction told me that confession was the best course. I sighed and said, "When we lined up for that photo yesterday, I felt ugly, fat, and old." I didn't dare include "short." I'm so over it.

Andi shook her head fiercely. "You need to tell me about UFO sightings. Grab me the moment it happens, and say, 'Andi. UFO,' and I'll set you straight." She continued shaking her head and scowled at me like only a true friend can.

"UFO sighting?"

"Ugly. Fat. Old."

I laughed out loud.

"Your UFO sighting was a lie." Andi tried to look stern, but I could see the smile in her eyes. "I mean it, sissy. If you ever feel that way again, you'd better tell me so I can remind you how beautiful you are."

In that moment, one of my divinely powered weapons popped into my head: "Let the king be enthralled by your beauty; honor him, for he is your lord" (Ps. 45:11 NIV). I thank God for recalling to mind the perfect Bible verse to counter my "less than" mindset.

I'm also thankful for friends who help me identify lies that keep me from living in freedom. I renounce the UFO lie and refuse to accept its cold prickly sting.

Are you still holding onto any cold pricklies? Seek out a trusted friend who can spot it and knock it loose. And please don't forget about the worksheets in the appendix. Guiding you to them is my way of handing you warm fuzzies. I encourage you to spend time completing both activities so that you can identify and renounce every lie you fall for. God will reveal the verses that best serve you as divinely powered weapons. Wield God's Word like a sword to defeat dangerous lies like false UFO sightings. Believe truth. Speak life.

Ask any champion, and they will tell you that keeping the victor's title takes as much effort as winning it in the first place. One way to ensure you continue to walk in victory is to pray David's prayer from Psalm 139:23–24. Asking God to search you, test you, and expose any offenses will help keep you courageous, humble, and yielded to the will of God.

Step Over Offenses

I thank God for patiently investing the time needed to teach me to listen for and discern his voice. You can hear from God too. Your faithfulness in studying Psalm 139—wholly expectant that God will speak—has tuned your ear to his voice. This ability provides huge benefits because God speaks for good reasons. He offers wisdom, knowledge, and understanding. He also issues commands and gives guidance. Learning to recognize God's whispers and follow his directions saved me from the full gut-punch impact of rejection the day I left the job I held for nearly five years.

The department I worked in shared a floor with another department, and each had an employee leaving the same day. A sign-up sheet circulated the floor to bring food for a good-bye celebration honoring the two of us. I wondered whether to bring something to my own party and felt God direct me to give each of my coworkers a blessing—as in the five-step Hebrew blessing I shared in Chapter Three. (Under the circumstances, I selectively included the meaningful touch and excluded the active commitment component.)

I prayed for my coworkers by name, and God led me to purchase a unique gift for each one. He also gave me specific words of blessing for them. I followed all his directions and joyfully prepared my good-bye gifts. I arrived early to bring the wrapped packages to the good-bye celebration and waited with anticipation for my coworkers to arrive.

The room began to fill with people. All but one were from the other department. And the young woman from my department worked in a different division. I had prepared a verbal blessing for her and my other colleagues in her division, but had purchased gifts exclusively for people in my own division. I planned to distribute the gifts first, so I waited. At one point, my boss came into the room. He picked up a paper plate, filled it with food, and left.

As time ticked away, I realized that no one from my department was going to show up.

The sole attendee from my department returned to her desk, and the room emptied. I scooped up all my brightly wrapped presents and took them back to my desk. I had already removed the pictures from my office walls and boxed up the personal belongings that once filled my workspace with joy.

My bare surroundings accentuated the naked realization that no one on my team had come to say good-bye or wish me success in my new endeavors. I took a moment to talk myself off the ledge of rejection and then popped in on my coworkers one by one.

I watched them open their gifts while I shared a personal blessing. When I poked my head into the office of the young woman who had been at the party, I thanked her for coming and carefully selected my words to let her know that I had planned on blessing her then but missed the opportunity.

By the time I visited my boss, I had acquired a clear assessment of what had happened that afternoon. He had assigned workloads that kept most of my coworkers from attending. Sensing the tension in my boss's office when I arrived with his gift, I quickly identified the root of the afternoon's offense. Those awkward moments taught me not to confuse *being* rejected with *feeling* rejected.

If we allow legitimate feelings of rejection to trick us into acting on false assumptions, we risk damaging positive, healthy relationships. The sting of being left out may at times be symptomatic of benign circumstances. I think of one coworker in particular who grew misty eyed when she opened her gift and whispered her regret at not being able to attend the good-bye party.

I had expected my boss to do for me what he had done for every other employee who left the organization during my tenure—complete with speeches and a gift card. The reasons why I was treated differently had far more to do with him than me.

Though I chose not to take offense at the role my boss played in making me feel insignificant, I didn't get over the pain of his disregard quickly. I had to be intentional about forgiving him. I had to spend time in prayer, asking God to heal the hurt caused by my boss's neglect.

I love the poetry of the King James Version. No other version of the Bible translates Psalm 119:165 quite like King James, which says, "Great peace have they which love thy law: and nothing shall offend them." The word "offend" in the original Hebrew is *mikshol*. The *New Strong's Complete Dictionary* defines *mikshol* as "a stumbling-block, literally or figuratively (obstacle, enticement [specifically an idol], scruple)—caused to fall, offence."

Looking backward at past offenses will cause us to stumble as we move forward. You can't walk in victory when offenses trip you up. If offenses block your path, please refer to the Prayer of Forgiveness at the end of Chapter Four. Roll the stumbling block away, release your offender to God, and renounce your right to judge or seek revenge.

Resist the devil by refusing to allow bitterness into the emptiness hollowed out by an offense. Overcome evil with good by blessing the people who offend you—if not to their faces then within your heart. Rise above the ground war by stepping over an offense.

Choosing to walk in victory doesn't mean stumbling blocks will never roll onto your path. You may stub your toe on a painful offense from time to time. Choose to stay close to God. Allow him to search and expose you.

If you've been the offender, take immediate steps to remove the obstacle you dropped in another's path. Seek forgiveness and return to God. He will lead you up and over each offense along the path of everlasting life.

Step Up to Acceptance

In the earliest days of the church, the apostles held a narrow view about who could enter the kingdom of God. Jesus enlarged their perspective as he walked with them on earth. Women and children were every bit as precious in his sight as men. Tax collectors and sinners were no less welcome to dine with him than devout Jews. Even a Canaanite woman from a pagan culture received the healing she sought from Jesus because of her great faith.

After Jesus ascended into heaven, he relied on the Holy Spirit to continue enlarging the apostles' perspective of who could enter the kingdom of God.

Peter had been one of Jesus's closest friends on earth. Jesus called him a rock and said he would build his church on that rock. Peter's church-building assignment called for a comprehensive view of exactly who God deemed acceptable. No prejudice could hold Peter back from sharing how to get right with God.

The early church thought that only Jews could become Christians. Sadly, today's church also has preconceived ideas about who is acceptable to God. If you think only certain people from certain backgrounds can come to Jesus, I recommend you read the whole story of Peter's visit with a Roman army officer named Cornelius. The fascinating account in Acts 10 opens with Cornelius seeing an angel coming toward him and calling him by name. Cornelius stared in shock and terror. Why would an angel approach a Gentile? Cornelius's fear must have turned to curiosity when the angel commended him for giving to the poor and instructed him to send for Peter.

Cornelius immediately sent two of his servants and one of his personal assistants to bring Peter from Joppa, a day's journey away. As they neared the seaside city, Peter was in the midst of having his own perplexing vision. Rather than seeing an angel, Peter saw a sheet filled with animals lowered before him. His vision replayed three times and came with a command from heaven: "Do not call something unclean if God has made it clean." The strange sight prepared Peter for the invitation he was about to receive to the home of a Gentile.

I love how God works both ends and leaves it up to us to meet in the middle. Peter accepted the invitation to visit Cornelius and learned that God's gift of eternal life is available to *all* who believe. As detailed in Acts 10:1–35, after watching Cornelius and his household accept the gospel message and receive the Holy

Spirit, Peter said, "I see very clearly that God shows no favoritism. In every nation he accepts those who fear him and do what is right."

Peter witnessed firsthand that *all* who believe in Jesus will have their sins forgiven. Subsequently, he built the church on the premise that God accepts *all* people in *every* nation who fear him and do what is right. And just to be clear about what is "right," Paul's letter to the Romans—the church to which Cornelius clearly belonged—explained that no one can ever be made right with God through works or obedience. Romans 3:22 says, "We are made right with God by placing our faith in Jesus Christ. And this is true for everyone who believes, no matter who we are."

Satan knows that the blood of Jesus covers the sin of everyone who believes, no matter who they are. But he perpetuates the lie that some sins can't be covered. My heart breaks for those deceived by the lie that God doesn't accept *all* who place their faith in Jesus Christ.

Whether bent low with shame or puffed up with self-righteous pride, they are wrong to believe that confessing Jesus as Lord and Savior isn't enough. *No one* accepted by God through Jesus Christ has made too many mistakes to belong and be loved. One of the most familiar verses in all of Scripture says it best:

> For God so loved the world that he gave his one and
> only Son, that whoever believes in him shall not perish
> but have eternal life. (John 3:16 NIV)

Key words: WHOEVER BELIEVES. Period.

One of the saddest Bible verses I've ever read is found in 2 Corinthians 4:4:

> Satan, who is the god of this world, has blinded the
> minds of those who don't believe. They are unable to see

the glorious light of the Good News. They don't understand this message about the glory of Christ, who is the
exact likeness of God.

I see the reality of this tragedy daily. I want to help people see Jesus,
but I can't do that if I'm stuck in a pit of rejection. The isolation and
emptiness make me too needy. My pastor once drew a vivid word
picture that convicted me. He said, "I can walk into a room and
say, 'Here I am,' or I can walk in saying, 'There you are.'"

While I don't know your story, I've tried to keep your coun-
tenance and your longing to belong ever before me as I write.
Certainly outcasts like the Samaritan woman and Rahab experienced rejection. But so did heroes like Joshua and Queen Esther.
Their stories differ, but their happy endings were authored by the
same God. He is writing your story too.

I think it's safe to assume that you are open to pursuing spiritual and emotional health through Biblical affirmations. While it's
entirely possible you've suffered rejection at the hands of people
professing to follow Jesus, the fact that you've read this far means
you aren't hostile toward the message of Jesus Christ.

A few years ago, I spoke at a women's retreat hosted by a
Christian denomination that generally doesn't share my views on
some hot-button issues. They invited me to teach spiritual and
practical ways to hear the voice of God. It probably won't surprise
you that I taught them the look, list, learn, listen, and live journaling method.

During the course of the weekend, we used the five-step
formula to work through John 10:1–15.

Several women approached me throughout the conference
with their opinions—from the woman who graciously taxied
me from the airport to the conference center to the woman who
returned me to the airport for my flight home. All questioned me

about my views on those hot-button issues. Each time, I answered to the best of my ability from Scripture. In other words, I didn't say "I think" or "I believe." I said, "The Bible says . . . ." I've never felt more challenged as a teacher. Only one woman shared my views.

Just prior to my departure from the conference center, a woman chased me down for a hug. "Shawna, I disagree with you about almost everything, but I love what you taught us about how to hear from God." She pulled out the journal she had received at the conference and began flipping through the pages. "I'm going to start reading the Bible every day, and I'm going to use this journal. I've never studied the Bible before, and I'm looking forward to listening to what God has to say."

Her enthusiasm replenished my depleted energy reserves. I had poured myself out, determined to point women with diverse viewpoints to God, the source of all wisdom and truth. I would always choose to have someone listen to and agree with God over listening to and agreeing with me. My goal that weekend had never been to change opinions on hot-button issues or encourage tolerance of my view. I went to share the unconditional love of God and to invite women to accept all he has done for them.

Acceptance isn't the same as tolerance. I prefer being accepted to being tolerated. *Tolerance* refers to a permissive attitude toward opinions, beliefs, and practices that differ from one's own. God doesn't *tolerate* you, me, or anyone else.

Jesus taught that whoever does not believe in him stands condemned. To some, that may sound intolerant. In truth, God has thrown open the door to the kingdom of heaven. Yes, Jesus is the way, the truth, and the life, and no one can come to the Father except through him. But *anyone* can come to Jesus.

Don't settle for tolerance when Jesus offers ultimate acceptance. Come to Jesus. Be accepted. Walk in victory!

Chapter Nine

THE KEY TO FREEDOM

I followed a young woman into the gym recently. She wore a racer-back shirt designed for freedom of movement. As she paused at the counter to flash her membership ID, I squinted to read the tattoo on her left shoulder blade. The pretty cursive letters tattooed at a slight upward angle read, "I am fearfully and wonderfully made. Psalm 139." I smiled at her obvious commitment to declaring her true identity.

You were designed for freedom of movement too. Trying to walk in victory while bound by chains of insecurity or inadequacy is like trying to lift weights with your arms shackled to a wall. Break free of every chain that keeps you from the joy of acceptance. Permanently imprint upon your heart and mind (body optional) the truth of your identity and incredible worth.

God knows me.

He is always with me.

I am not invisible.

I am wonderfully made.

God's countless thoughts are for me.

I have enemies, but . . .

I can walk in victory!

We've nearly reached the end of our quest to discover the joy of acceptance. But our journey wouldn't be complete without a sketch of David, the author of Psalm 139 who lived every divinely inspired word of its twenty-four verses.

David's father relegated him to lowly shepherd boy, but God knew his potential for greatness. David's family included members who turned against him, but God stayed with him continually. David's body and soul fell into temptation and sin, but God thought of him as a man after his own heart. David's enemies attacked from outside Israel's borders and attempted coups from within, but God established his throne forever. David's epic life illustrates the truth of the Manifesto of Acceptance.

God knows me.

He is always with me.

I am not invisible.

I am wonderfully made.

God's countless thoughts are for me.

I have enemies, but . . .

I can walk in victory!

David's story contrasts human failures with God's faithfulness. Let's take a look at how he became Israel's king and how his forty-year reign ended.

The Father's Choice

History has a way of repeating itself. Sadly, daddy issues can have a long history. David nearly handed down to his son Solomon the same curse of rejection his father dealt him—albeit unintentionally. Thankfully, both David and his father, Jesse, proved human neglect never nullifies our Heavenly Father's acceptance.

David's story begins when God sent his prophet Samuel to David's home in Bethlehem. As chronicled in 1 Samuel 16, God said to Samuel, "You have mourned long enough for Saul. I have rejected him as king of Israel, so fill your flask with olive oil and go to Bethlehem. Find a man named Jesse who lives there, for I have selected one of his sons to be my king."

Samuel invited Jesse and all Jesse's sons to a purification rite, but David's daddy didn't bother to bring his youngest son. Samuel took one look at his eldest and thought, "Surely this is the LORD's anointed." But the Lord said to Samuel, "Don't judge by his appearance or height, for I have rejected him. The LORD doesn't see things the way you see them. People judge by outward appearance, but the LORD looks at the heart."

Jesse asked the next oldest to step forward, but Samuel said the Lord had not chosen him either. So Jesse summoned his third-born son. The Bible says, "In the same way *all* seven of Jesse's sons were presented to Samuel. But Samuel said to Jesse, 'The LORD has not chosen any of these.' Then Samuel asked, 'Are these all the sons you have?'

"'There is still the youngest,' Jesse replied. '*But* he's out in the fields watching the sheep and goats.'"

In these verses, I italicized the two words that frustrate me. Jesse didn't present *all* his sons, and when Samuel called him on it, he said, "*But . . . .*" Jesse's ready reason for not inviting David proves intent. He didn't forget about his youngest; he purposefully ignored him.

Samuel would not be moved from anointing God's choice. He insisted Jesse send for David immediately, saying, "We will not sit down to eat until he arrives."

The Bible doesn't say how David reacted as he finally stood among his brothers and Samuel anointed him as king. However, the story of David's encounter with Goliath in 1 Samuel 17:26–28 indicates how his oldest brother, Eliab, may have felt.

Sent by Jesse with food to the frontlines of the battle against the Philistines, young David arrived, saw the taunting giant, and asked, "What will a man get for killing this Philistine and ending his defiance of Israel? Who is this pagan Philistine anyway, that he is allowed to defy the armies of the living God?"

Eliab heard David questioning the nearby soldiers and became angry. "What are you doing around here anyway?" he demanded. "What about those few sheep you're supposed to be taking care of? I know about your pride and deceit. You just want to see the battle!"

Scripture does not support Eliab's assessment of his little brother. Quite the opposite, David was a man after God's own heart. He killed Goliath that day, but intermingled with the memory of his victory against the giant, he certainly remembered the belittling comments spat at him by Eliab. David rose to the position of Israel's king on the firm foundation of God's anointing but also the shaky ground of familial rejection.

David's personal experience of being ignored by family in his youth manifested in his adulthood with his own "out of sight, out of mind" parenting style. He did not intervene in the lives of his children, instead turning a blind eye to issues as tragic as rape and murder (2 Sam. 13). He also failed to take timely action naming the successor to his throne.

In 1 Kings 1:15–35, David was old, weak, and most likely bed-ridden when Bathsheba, his wife and the mother of Solomon, came into his bedroom and bowed down before him saying, "My lord, you made a vow before the LORD your God when you said to me, 'Your son Solomon will surely be the next king and will sit on my throne.' But instead, Adonijah has made himself king, and my lord the king does not even know about it." Here, Bathsheba references Adonijah, one of David's sons from a different mother. "And now, my lord the king, all Israel is waiting for you to announce who will become king after you. If you do not act, my son Solomon and I will be treated as criminals as soon as my lord the king has died."

David had just heard Bathsheba's news when Nathan the prophet appeared before him. "My lord the king, have you decided that Adonijah will be the next king and that he will sit on your throne?" Nathan reported the celebration Adonijah hosted and the people in attendance. "They are feasting and drinking with him and shouting, 'Long live King Adonijah!' . . . Has my lord the king really done this without letting any of his officials know who should be the next king?"

Once made aware of his near disastrous neglect, David took immediate action. First, he gave Bathsheba this vow: "As surely as the LORD lives, who has rescued me from every danger, your son Solomon will be the next king and will sit on my throne this very day, just as I vowed to you before the LORD, the God of Israel." Then, he ordered his officials to anoint Solomon king over Israel. David said to Nathan and the officials, "Blow the ram's horn and shout, 'Long live King Solomon!' Then escort him back here, and he will sit on my throne. He will succeed me as king, for I have appointed him to be ruler over Israel and Judah."

David's commands quickly ended Adonijah's celebration. Once again, God's plan had not been thwarted. Be encouraged by God's intervention in David's life. No daddy issues with an earthly father can keep you "out of sight, out of mind" with your Heavenly Father. Declare our Manifesto of Acceptance to seal that truth in your heart and mind.

God knows me.

He is always with me.

I am not invisible.

I am wonderfully made.

God's countless thoughts are for me.

I have enemies, but . . .

I can walk in victory!

God stands ready to intervene on your behalf. At any time, he can go from waiting in the wings to taking center stage. Do you remember our secret signal? I encourage you to point to yourself, and then reach for your pointer finger and pull it straight up. Declare your value as you give the *I'm Special Sisterhood* sign, and imagine God lifting you into the spotlight of his love.

Nothing can nullify God's acceptance of you. Not even a father's neglect. Forget failed attempts to win favor from your dad or any other hard-to-please person. Rest in the prized identity that belongs to you in Christ.

You are special. Don't ever forget it.

Labeling Your Key

I long to give you the same token I gave the women who attended the Bible study that launched the book you hold. The last day of class, they each received an old-style, copper-colored key that measured about the breadth of your hand. As I did with the virtual flower at the start of our journey, I am placing this key into your hands right now. Close your eyes for a moment and receive it.

You have mastered the art of believing and speaking truth with power and authority.

You have identified supernatural keys from the Bible that open doors to a life of freedom and acceptance.

You are fully equipped to break free of rejection and claim your rightful place of belonging.

As you feel the weight of the ornate key pressed into your palm, wrap your fingers around its role as a reminder to lock up lies and unlock truth. I want to be as pragmatic as possible by helping you discern exactly what thoughts and behaviors your key locks and unlocks.

Which supernatural keys collected from your journal and worksheets do you *most* want to remember?

Which reminder will help you stay true to right thinking and right standing?

Which word or phrase will unlock the truth of your extreme value and esteemed identity?

In order to lock away lies that keep you from living in freedom, you must identify and renounce every wrong belief. The key I placed in your hand can help you take captive each lie you hear or think or say about who you are and what you have to offer. In order to cancel the negative effects of those lies and establish yourself with right standing, you must believe and speak truth. Your key can unlock shackles of past rejections and swing open doors to victorious living. You are a member of the *I'm Special Sisterhood* with every right to bask in the joy of knowing that your deepest longings have been satisfied.

You are beautiful.

You belong.

You are loved!

Picture the copper-colored key I pressed into your palm. Imagine yourself threading a piece of twine through the loop at the top of the key's decorative head. The twine holds a plain brown tag to label your key.

What message of freedom will you write on your tag?

What thoughts and behaviors does your key lock and unlock?

What word or phrase will remind you of your constant, easy access to God's acceptance?

To help determine your personal label, consider what you would write in the following blanks.

I would not be bound up by rejection if only . . .

- I could have an abundance of _____.
- I always remembered that I am _____.
- I never hesitated to be _____.

I would be free to be myself and know that I am accepted if only . . .

- I could describe myself as _____.
- I had the faith and courage to _____.
- I could count on myself to always _____.

Completing your journal and worksheets gave you opportunities to fulfill every "if only." No obstacle stands between you and acceptance. Perhaps you identify with the obstacles that hindered the Bible characters I highlighted in the various sketches throughout. Each character overcame difficult circumstances by adding faith to fear and pairing courage with action. If you relate to their struggles, you might gain access to your place of belonging with the same key truths they grasped. Consider whether one of the following keys will help you lock the door to a life of defeat and open for you a life blessed with acceptance.

1. **The Woman at the Well**
   Right thinking: God knows me.
   Right standing: I know who I am in Christ. Therefore I won't let the opinions and behaviors of others define me.
   Keys to freedom may include: unconditional love, adequacy, validation, significance

2. **Joshua**
   Right thinking: He is always with me.
   Right standing: I know God will never abandon me. Therefore I won't fear loneliness, isolation, or betrayal.
   Keys to freedom may include: courage, boldness, confidence, stability

3. **Rahab**
   Right thinking: I am not invisible.
   Right standing: I know God sees me. Therefore I

renounce my right to judge or seek revenge, and I
release my offenders to God.

Keys to freedom may include: forgiveness, well-placed
trust, healthy relationships, pure intimacy

4. **Esther**

Right thinking: I am wonderfully made.

Right standing: I know God designed me for a unique
purpose. Therefore I refuse to feel unwanted or less
than, and I declare that I am desirable and enough.

Keys to freedom may include: competence, transparency,
satisfaction, strong self-image

5. **Joseph**

Right thinking: God's countless thoughts are for me.

Right standing: I know God hasn't forgotten me.
Therefore I will hold onto God's promises in spite of
contradicting circumstances.

Keys to freedom may include: enduring faith, patience,
perseverance, contentment

6. **Woman with Constant Bleeding**

Right thinking: I have enemies, but . . .

Right standing: I know I have power and authority in
Christ. Therefore I won't fight like the world does but
will use divine weapons to demolish strongholds.

Keys to freedom may include: a heart of worship, expectancy, resilience, persistence

7. **Paul**

Right thinking: I can walk in victory!

Right standing: I know I must choose to overcome by
faith. Therefore I will keep an eternal perspective
regarding wins and losses.

Keys to freedom may include: resolve, fortitude, security,
assurance

8. **David**

> Right thinking: I'm special.
>
> Right standing: I know I am treasured as a beloved child of God. Therefore I won't allow my past to control my future.
>
> Keys to freedom may include: full of potential, self-worth, optimism, unashamed

These examples, together with the "if only" statements above, are intended to help you discern how to label your key. Now is the time to ask God to reveal your personal message of freedom. What will you write on the virtual tag of your copper-colored key?

Close your eyes once more and make a fist around that imaginary key in your hand. Wait on the voice of God to whisper your unique key to freedom.

When you know what it is, please write it down like this:

My key to freedom is _____.

Put it on a 3 × 5 card. Print it across the front of your journal. Tattoo it on your heart and mind. Keep your key truths ever before you. Carry your message of freedom as a reminder that you never have to go looking for acceptance. You are a precious child of God. He knit you together with precision and excellence, and he accepts you just the way you are.

Opening Doors with Your Key

Now that you've climbed out of the pit of an unmet longing, you have more to offer than you realize. I prayed for you to receive such an infilling of the Holy Spirit that you pour acceptance into others out of the overflow. You have so much to offer this broken world.

I can see my pastor delivering the word picture I gave earlier. He stood on the platform in front of our church, arms folded, head cocked to one side, and said, "I can walk into a room and say, 'Here I am.'" He flung his arms open wide and struck a ta-dah pose. After pausing for effect, he took a step forward and extended his arms toward us in a warm, welcoming gesture. Then said, "Or I can walk in saying, 'There you are.'"

Rejection says, "Here I am," too. But rather than declaring it with a prideful "ta-dah," rejection whispers its longing to be seen. Acceptance satisfies that longing. Knowing we belong makes us less susceptible to the sting of rejection. Knowing we belong frees us to say, "There you are." Satan knows this and doesn't want us to know that we belong. He uses rejection to make us sit down and shut up.

When Jesus called Peter a rock and said he would build his church on that rock, he also that his church would be "so expansive with energy that not even the gates of hell will be able to keep it out. And that's not all. You will have complete and free access to God's kingdom, keys to open any and every door: no more barriers between heaven and earth, earth and heaven." (Matt. 16:18–19 MSG).

I love this promise!

The church has the power to storm the gates of hell and snatch people from the fire. No wonder Satan tries to convince us we are insignificant and powerless. He is dead wrong.

You have life-giving power in your tiny tongue.

You hold the keys of the kingdom of heaven.

You can open doors for others trapped by Satan's lies.

With the power and authority you have in Jesus Christ, you can tell Satan to sit down and shut up. Hallelujah!

Guard the truth you hold. Never surrender ground through wrong thinking and wrong standing. Continue reading the Bible and asking God to reveal spiritual wisdom and knowledge. Continue journaling what you hear from God. Continue believing and speaking the truth about your identity and worth. Now that you've discovered the joy of acceptance, nothing can keep you from walking in victory. You hold the keys, sister. This is your time!

Appendix

TOOLS TO BELIEVE AND SPEAK TRUTH

Journaling Instructions

Five words—look, list, learn, listen, and live—guide the method I use to tune my ears to the right frequency to hear from God. I modeled this five-step formula for meditating on Scriptures after a method I learned from Anne Graham Lotz. I'm convinced that journaling in this way turns up the volume of God's still, small voice. Here's how to begin:

1. Purchase either a spiral bound notebook or a hardbound composition book (college-ruled).
2. Remove the explanation of the five-step formula that follows these instructions (entitled "My Journal of Psalm 139") from this book, and paste it onto the first page of your journal, opposite the inside of the cover.
3. Turn the page so that you have blank pages on the left and right. You will complete your journaling activities on two-page spreads.
4. High in the top margin of the left-hand page, write LOOK, and record the verses you are about to study (for example, "LOOK: Psalm 139:1–4").

5. Divide the left-hand page into two columns. Label them in the top margin by writing LIST in the left column and LEARN in the right column.
6. In the same way, divide the right-hand page into two columns. Label the left column LISTEN and the right column LIVE.
7. Use the columns to write your responses to the remaining four steps in the formula.

My Journal of Psalm 139

FIVE-STEP FORMULA:
Look, List, Learn, Listen, and Live

1. **LOOK** AT THE WORD: PRAY BEFORE I BEGIN.
   Read the assigned verses from Psalm 139. Underline, circle, or otherwise mark the text in any way if it will aid in my study.

2. **LIST** THE FACTS: WHAT DOES IT SAY?
   Make a verse-by-verse list of the most outstanding, obvious facts. Be literal as I pare down the text and write what the verses say.

3. **LEARN** FROM THE LESSONS: WHAT DOES IT MEAN?
   Consider the spiritual principles taught by the verses. Write any promises to claim, warnings to heed, commands to obey, and examples to follow or avoid.

4. **LISTEN** TO HIS VOICE: WHAT DOES IT MEAN TO ME?
   Consider again the spiritual principles, but this time focus on how the lessons apply directly to me. Frame the lessons into questions that prompt personal reflection, as if God were speaking to me. Listen for a loving voice that offers hope with no condemnation.

5. **LIVE** IN RESPONSE: WHAT WILL I DO ABOUT IT?
   Reflect on my responses to the questions. Pinpoint what to do with the knowledge God has revealed to me. Be specific as I journal what God is challenging me to believe and speak. Consider writing this response as a prayer of commitment to trust and obey God. Record today's date.

Who *I AM* Is and Who I Am

This activity is designed to help you:

- Magnify your knowledge of the character of God
- Expand your comprehension of what God says about you
- Equip yourself to disallow anyone apart from God to define you
- Claim your rightful place of belonging as a beloved child of God
- Memorize and recite verses that lead you into the joy of acceptance

Creating Your Worksheet

1. I consider this activity another journaling assignment, so I recommend finding some blank pages in your journal.
2. Identify Bible verses that contradict what you currently believe about yourself and/or God. Please visit ShawnaMarieBryant.com/WhoIAm for assistance finding these verses.
3. Choose a verse that will help you believe and speak truth, and write it in your journal. Directly beneath the verse, write a brief statement acknowledging the lies you believed and explaining why you no longer believe them.
4. Memorize the verse so you can recite it when needed to counter any lies you're tempted to believe.
5. Repeat steps 3–4 with as many different verses as you need.

Sample Worksheet

Who I AM is:

God is not a man, so he does not lie. He is not human, so he does not change his mind. Has he ever spoken and failed to act? Has he ever promised and not carried it through?
—Numbers 23:19

I can't compare God to anyone. He's unlike anyone I've met, even the best person I know. God doesn't lie, so I can trust him. He will never break a promise to me.

Who I AM is:

This is what the LORD says—the LORD who made the earth, who formed and established it, whose name is the LORD: Ask me and I will tell you remarkable secrets you do not know about things to come.
—Jeremiah 33:2–3

I don't have to wonder about what God wants or expects of me. He doesn't leave me in the dark. He is in charge of all creation and has all the answers. All I have to do is ask him, and he will tell me what I need to know.

Who I am:

Yet to all who did receive him, to those who believed in his name, he gave the right to become children of God—children born not of natural descent, nor of human decision or a husband's will, but born of God.
—John 1:12–13 NIV

The family I was born into and the way I was raised don't determine whether I'm part of God's family. I am a child of God because I received Jesus. As his child, I have all the rights that come with being a family member by birth. I belong to the same family as the King of kings! That makes me royalty.

Who I AM is:

I have loved you even as the Father has loved me. Remain in my love. When you obey my commandments, you remain in my love, just as I obey my Father's commandments and remain in his love. I have told you these things so that you will be filled with my joy. Yes, your joy will overflow!
—John 15:9–11

God is not a mean or strict disciplinarian. I don't have to prove myself for him to accept me. Obedience to God doesn't make him love me more. Jesus loves me like the Father loves his Son. I am loved because I'm a child of God. Obeying God keeps me closer to the love he already has for me. Obedience isn't a joy killer. Obeying God makes my joy overflow.

Who I am:

But you are not like that, for you are a chosen people. You are royal priests, a holy nation, God's very own possession. As a result, you can show others the goodness of God, for he called you out of the darkness into his wonderful light. "Once you had no identity as a people; now you are God's people. Once you received no mercy; now you have received God's mercy."

—1 Peter 2:9–10

I am not an outsider who doesn't belong. I am part of something so much bigger than myself. I am chosen. I am holy. I belong in the light.

What I Thought versus What I Know

This activity is designed to help you:

- Call out negative thinking patterns
- Expose lies you have believed about yourself
- Equip you with divinely powered weapons from Scripture
- Cancel the negative effects of lies by believing and speaking truth
- Bring your feelings about yourself into alignment with how God feels about you

Creating Your Worksheet

1. This is another great exercise to do in your journal. Find a page and divide it into two columns. The left column should take up only 25 percent of the page. Make the right column three times the size.
2. Label the left column "What I Thought (Lies)." Label the right column, "What I Know (Truth)."
3. In the left column, write down negative things that you think or say about yourself.
4. Identify Bible verses that affirm your value, and in the right-hand column, write them alongside the related self-destructive statements. Please visit ShawnaMarieBryant.com/WhoIAm for assistance finding these verses.
5. Scripture has divine power to demolish strongholds. When you find yourself believing the lies listed on the left, declare the verses written beside those wrong beliefs. This practice helps you take your thoughts captive.

Sample Worksheet

What I Thought (Lies)	What I Know (Truth)
I'm stupid.	*If you need wisdom, ask our generous God, and he will give it to you. He will not rebuke you for asking.* —James 1:5 *For the LORD grants wisdom! From his mouth come knowledge and understanding.... For wisdom will enter your heart, and knowledge will fill you with joy.* —Proverbs 2:6, 10
No one cares about me.	*I have loved you even as the Father has loved me. Remain in my love.* —John 15:9 *See what great love the Father has lavished on us, that we should be called children of God! And that is what we are! The reason the world does not know us is that it did not know him.* —1 John 3:1 NIV *The LORD appeared to us in the past, saying: "I have loved you with an everlasting love; I have drawn you with unfailing kindness."* —Jeremiah 31:3 NIV
My feelings don't matter.	*Can a mother forget the baby at her breast and have no compassion on the child she has borne? Though she may forget, I will not forget you! See, I have engraved you on the palms of my hands; your walls are ever before me.* —Isaiah 49:15–16 NIV *Give all your worries and cares to God, for he cares about you.* —1 Peter 5:7

Acknowledgments

My women's ministry director, Joni Oquist, took me to lunch one day to share her desire to offer a second women's Bible study on Wednesday nights. She invited me to teach any subject for any duration. With this honor came responsibility, so I asked God what topic I should teach. He replied with one word: rejection. I wanted to run from that abhorrent word. Instead, I yielded to God, who began revealing deep truths from Psalm 139. If it wasn't for Joni, this book might not be in your hands. Thank you, Joni, for providing the platform on which I humbly stand.

In spring 2002, after leading nine worship gatherings over three days at a conference center in the Santa Cruz mountains, I was headed for an afternoon nap when God redirected me. I reluctantly changed course and found myself in a workshop led by an insightful intercessor named Cosey Odom. She anointed me with oil that day, and confirmed God's call on my life to speak and write for his glory. Cosey has prayed for nearly twenty years for God's will to be accomplished in me. If it wasn't for her, I could've easily abandoned my calling. Thank you, Cosey, for encouraging me to pursue it.

I attended my first writers' conference in 2005 with my friend Kim Bagato and a shared dream to write. We met fellow attendees

Carrie Padgett and Dot Powell, and the four of us immediately formed a writers' critique group. Kim and Carrie still belonged to our little group when I began bringing the pages that would fill this book. By then, Andi Bull and Kelly Hollman had joined us. If it wasn't for these gifted women, I would not consider my writing good enough to get published and would've given up on my dream. Thank you, ladies, for making me a better, more confident writer.

As I write this, my precious mom, Marilyn Kirkwood, is receiving hospice care and anticipating heaven—home to my dad, Bruce Kirkwood, and my first (and longest in duration) weekly prayer partner, Kieffer Lehman, who died ten years to the day after my dad and was like a second father to me. More than anyone else, these saints taught me the value of consistently bowing, one-on-one, in prayer to move mountainous obstacles and unleash boundless blessings.

Powerful women who have met regularly with me for the primary purpose of prayer include Sharon Zeigler, who laid hands on my belly soon after I conceived my firstborn and has prayed with me through life's highs and lows ever since; Miriam Bennett, who gave me a reason to rise before the sun to place a free phone call back when phone service charged by the minute; Donita Warren, who frequently fed me and my family spiritual food and homemade bread; Leticia Alverez, who introduced herself as one appointed by God to pray me to the next level of my calling and faithfully kept her assignment; and Toby Delaney, who has a room in her home set apart for prayers that not only touch heaven but also rattle hell. If it wasn't for these prayer warriors, I would not know that Fear + Faith = Courage and Courage + Action = Victory. I also acknowledge my true friends who pray through my monthly prayer letter, and I salute my small group family for laughing and crying and doing life with me. Thank you, men and women of prayer, for keeping me from being too broken to be of any use to God.

I not only stand on the strong shoulders of my mom and dad; I also lean on the solid support of my family. Laurie Gabriel, my big sister and biggest fan, has believed in me since before I could walk; Sarah and Scott, my gorgeous and godly children, have made my life a joyous adventure that abounds with stories they permit me to share; and Steve, my beloved husband and backer upper, has faithfully walked alongside me over every mountain and through every valley in our marriage. Together victorious! Thank you, Laurie, Sarah, Scott, and Steve, for being the best family ever. I am proud to call you mine.

Notes

Chapter One: The Manifesto

[1] While I certainly invite men to use this material to devise a game plan to discover their inherent value, I originally wrote it for women's Bible study. Even though my sisters are my focus as I write, the techniques I share are not exclusively feminine. To my brothers who are brave enough to hold this book, I welcome you too. After all, the author of Psalm 139 was a man after God's own heart (see 1 Sam. 13:14 and Acts 13:22). Look to him and Jesus as your teachers.

[2] For a helpful video demonstration, visit http://www.handspeak.com.

[3] In 1997, I participated in a women's Bible study written by Anne Graham Lotz and learned the journaling technique I present in this book. I adopted it as my own but credit her for creating the simple formula I've followed for decades. See Anne Graham Lotz, *The Vision of His Glory* (Nashville: Word Publishing, 1996).

Chapter Two: God Knows Me

[1] Henry D. M. Spence, *The Complete Pulpit Commentary: Volume 7—Matthew to John* (Harrington, DE: Delmarva Publications, 2013), John 4:3. Original wording is in the public domain.

[2] Guy Winch, "Why We All Need to Practice Emotional First Aid," TEDxLinnaeusUniversity, November 2014, http://www.ted.com/talks/guy_winch_why_we_all_need_to_practice_emotional_first_aid?referrer=playlist-how_to_practice_emotional_first_aid.

[3] Lysa TerKeurst, *Uninvited: Living Loved When You Feel Less Than, Left Out, and Lonely* (Nashville: Nelson Books, 2016), 8.

[4] John Gill, "John Gill's Exposition of the Whole Bible," Bible Study Tools, Galatians 4:9, http://www.biblestudytools.com/commentaries/gills-exposition-of-the-bible/galatians-4-9.html, accessed December 19, 2019.

Chapter Three: He Is Always with Me

[1] Sarah Young, *Jesus Calling: Enjoying Peace in His Presence* (Nashville: Thomas Nelson, 2004), 174.

[2] Guy Winch, "Ten Surprising Facts about Rejection," *The Squeaky Wheel*, July 3, 2013, http://www.psychologytoday.com/us/blog/the-squeaky-wheel /201307/10-surprising-facts-about-rejection.

[3] Guy Winch, "Ten Surprising Facts about Rejection."

[4] TerKeurst, *Uninvited*, 94.

Chapter Four: I Am Not Invisible

[1] Henrike Moll and Allie Khalulyan, "'Not See, Not Hear, Not Speak': Preschoolers Think They Cannot Perceive or Address Others without Reciprocity," *Journal of Cognition and Development* 18, no. 1 (2017): 152–62.

[2] Stephen Marmer, "Forgiveness," PragerU.com, May 5, 2014, http://www .prageru.com/videos/forgiveness.

Chapter Five: I Am Wonderfully Made

[1] John Gill, "John Gill's Exposition of the Whole Bible," Bible Study Tools, Exodus 3:14, http://www.biblestudytools.com/commentaries/gills-exposition -of-the-bible/exodus-3-14.html, accessed December 19, 2019.

[2] Priscilla Shirer, video presentation of live speaking event retrieved from http://www.facebook.com/chuckbernal/videos/10156776390602915, accessed February 25, 2019.

[3] Christine Thomasos, "Priscilla Shirer Explains Stance on Racial and Christian Identity amid Backlash," AMBOtv Life Sermon Network, October 19, 2018, http://ambotv.com/blog/lifestyle/priscilla-shirer-explains-stance-on -racial-and-christian-identity-amid-backlash/.

Chapter Six: God's Countless Thoughts Are for Me

[1] This is a slogan of the United Negro College Fund (UNCF) from a fund-raising campaign launched in 1972 that is still in use today.

[2] TerKeurst, *Uninvited*, 47–48.

[3] John C. Maxwell, "John Maxwell: Six Tips to Develop and Model an Abundance Mindset," *Success*, March 4, 2015, http://www.success.com /john-c-maxwell-6-tips-to-develop-and-model-an-abundance-mindset/.

Chapter Eight: I Can Walk in Victory!

[1] Guy Winch, "Ten Surprising Facts about Rejection."